Palgrave Studies on Global Policy and Critical
Futures in Education

Series Editors
Michael Thomas
Liverpool John Moores University
Liverpool, UK

Jeffrey R. Di Leo
University of Houston-Victoria
Victoria, TX, USA

This transdisciplinary series investigates developments in the field of education in the age of neoliberalism, interrogating arguments and evidence for and against it as well as envisioning alternative educational futures. While much has been written about neoliberalism a key aim of the series is to explore and develop critical perspectives on how neoliberal and corporatist approaches have changed and impacted on educational institutions across all sectors, from schools to higher education, across the globe. The series engages with academics, researchers, curriculum developers, teachers, students and policy makers and provokes them to consider how neoliberal trends and values are affecting the direction of our educational institutions. Comparative studies with the US in particular as well as other prominent national and international contexts that have promoted these values will be encouraged alongside the UK, Australia and EU to identify the implications of recent policies, strategies and values on teaching, learning and research. Posing important questions and developing a critique around the need for evidence lies at the center of the series, which invites responses from advocates and proponents alike in order to shape an agenda which looks forward to making an impact on policy making. The series brings together a critical mass of evidence and aims to foster critical understanding and to understand the influence of neoliberal thinking on education in order to articulate alternative futures at this crucial moment when many professionals are deeply concerned about the developments taking place.

To submit a proposal, please contact the editors or commissioning editor:

Michael Thomas: m.thomas@ljmu.ac.uk and Jeffrey R. Di Leo: dileo@symploke.org

Milana Vernikova: Commissioning Editor, milana.vernikova@palgrave-usa.com

Gerbrand Tholen

The Role of Neoliberalism in the Marketisation of Higher Education

palgrave
macmillan

Gerbrand Tholen
Department of Sociology and Criminology
City St George's, University of London
London, UK

ISSN 2662-2246   ISSN 2662-2254 (electronic)
Palgrave Studies on Global Policy and Critical Futures in Education
ISBN 978-3-031-66280-5   ISBN 978-3-031-66281-2 (eBook)
https://doi.org/10.1007/978-3-031-66281-2

© Springer Nature Switzerland AG 2024

This work is subject to copyright. All rights are solely and exclusively licensed by the Publisher, whether the whole or part of the material is concerned, specifically the rights of translation, reprinting, reuse of illustrations, recitation, broadcasting, reproduction on microfilms or in any other physical way, and transmission or information storage and retrieval, electronic adaptation, computer software, or by similar or dissimilar methodology now known or hereafter developed.
The use of general descriptive names, registered names, trademarks, service marks, etc. in this publication does not imply, even in the absence of a specific statement, that such names are exempt from the relevant protective laws and regulations and therefore free for general use.
The publisher, the authors and the editors are safe to assume that the advice and information in this book are believed to be true and accurate at the date of publication. Neither the publisher nor the authors or the editors give a warranty, expressed or implied, with respect to the material contained herein or for any errors or omissions that may have been made. The publisher remains neutral with regard to jurisdictional claims in published maps and institutional affiliations.

Credit line: Jose A. Bernat Bacete/Getty Images

This Palgrave Macmillan imprint is published by the registered company Springer Nature Switzerland AG.
The registered company address is: Gewerbestrasse 11, 6330 Cham, Switzerland

If disposing of this product, please recycle the paper.

Contents

1	**Introduction**	1
	Neoliberalism	2
	Marketisation	4
	Marketisation as Neoliberalism	5
	Is It Really Neoliberalism?	7
	Rationale of the Book	8
	The Organisation of the Book	9
	References	10
2	**HE in Flux**	15
	Early Ideas	17
	Nineteenth Century	19
	The Non-instrumental Aim of Universities	22
	Educational Shift: Robbins and the 1960s	23
	Robbins: Intrinsic or Instrumental?	24
	After Robbins	26
	New Labour	27
	Tories: Cameron and May	30
	Conclusion: The Ideal of a University	32
	References	35

3 How Can We Understand Neoliberalism? 41
Short History of Neoliberal Thought 42
   Hayek and the Austrian School of Economics 44
   Chicago School and Friedman 47
   Friedman 48
   Public Choice 49
   Neoliberalism in Practice: Institution Building and Political Influence 51
How to Understand Neoliberalism 53
   Neoliberalism as Policy 54
   Neoliberalism as Ideology 57
   Neo-liberalism as Governmentality: Production of Neoliberal Subjectivity 60
Conclusion 64
References 66

4 How Has Neoliberalism Been Applied to HE? 71
Critique of Neoliberalism 73
   Neoliberalism Transforming Universities 74
   HE as a Private Good 75
   The Erosion of Academic Work 77
   Managerialism 78
Neoliberalism and HE 79
   Neoliberalism a Policy 79
   Neoliberalism as Ideology 80
   Neoliberalism as Governmentality 82
Conclusion 84
References 84

5 How Can We Understand the Role of Neoliberalism in the Marketisation of HE? 91
Marketisation 92
The Role of Markets 93
   Real Free Market? 94
   Private Good 97
   Quasi-Markets 98

The Role of Competition	100
Is It Neoliberal?	100
Finance and Fees	102
The Role of the State	104
Universities	108
Audit Practices	109
Managerialism	111
Students	112
Conclusion	113
References	114
6 Conclusion	**123**
Introduction	123
Key Points	125
Contributions to Our Understanding of Marketisation	125
What Does This Mean for Our Understanding of Neoliberalisation?	126
Neoliberalism as Policy	127
Neoliberalism as Ideology	128
Neoliberalisation as Governmentality	130
A New Approach: Neoliberalisation as a Wider Shift	131
Conclusion	134
References	135
References	**139**

CHAPTER 1

Introduction

Abstract This introductory chapter sets out the rationale of the book. Marketisation has affected the higher education sectors in many countries, and many have assumed that neoliberalism is the culprit. The chapter explains that we need to critically assess neoliberalism's role in the marketisation of higher education. It ends by setting out the organisation of the book.

Keywords Marketisation • Neoliberalism • Higher Education

Neoliberalism continues to be a popular concept to describe the social, political, and economic worlds around us. It has received a place in the modern lexicon and is used regularly in both popular writing and speech and academic writing. Specifically within the social sciences, the term has been used frequently (Venugopal, 2015), including to describe changes in education systems (Ingleby, 2021; Jones & Ball, 2023; Maisuria, 2014; Tett & Hamilton, 2021; etc.). For many observers, neoliberalism has impacted (public) education in many ways and is now entrenched within the system (Holmwood, 2011; Gerrard, 2015). In particular, higher education (HE) has been seen as undergoing a neoliberal transformation (Ball, 2015; Giroux, 2014; Mintz, 2021, etc.). Here, neoliberalism has

© The Author(s), under exclusive license to Springer Nature Switzerland AG 2024
G. Tholen, *The Role of Neoliberalism in the Marketisation of Higher Education*, Palgrave Studies on Global Policy and Critical Futures in Education, https://doi.org/10.1007/978-3-031-66281-2_1

been linked to a wide array of (mostly negative) developments ranging from reduced democratic decision making to diminished scholarship, from the decline of the humanities to the internationalisation of HE. Arguably, the clearest influence of neoliberalism is on the process of *marketisation*, in other words, the greater reliance on the use of markets in its management and functioning, applying the economic theory of the market to the provision of education (Brown, 2011a, p. 1). Where possible, a price mechanism balances supply and demand for university activities, most markedly education. Marketisation has been widely acknowledged as a driving force in modern HE systems (e.g. Brown, 2011b; Hill & Kumar, 2011; Lynch, 2006; McGettigan, 2013; Molesworth et al., 2010). It is noticeably expressed through national government policies, and some market principles have been observed to permeate HE systems worldwide. Examples are the pursuits of market and competition between universities and courses, transferring the cost of HE to students, and the student choice concept of customer-provider relationships in HE between students and institutions. Across the world, national HE sectors have experienced a gradual process of market introduction over the last decades (Williams, 2004; Foskett, 2011). Many governments have introduced reforms to increase market-led coordination of HE, balancing its provision through a price mechanism.

Through its pursuit of free markets and competition within all areas of life, particularly where the state currently intervenes, neoliberalism has often been seen as a primary force in marketisation. At first sight, the concept of neoliberalism seems to reflect the pervasive workings of the market in formerly non-market contexts, such as HE. However, upon closer inspection, neoliberalism is also associated with a whole range of other ideas and policies that do not directly fit marketisation in HE. Neoliberal theory emphasises how free markets serve as the optimum way of solving (social) problems and organising society, yet neoliberalism is more than merely pro-market. This book will assess how and to what extent marketisation in HE is driven by what we call neoliberalism. How useful is the concept of neoliberalism in explaining why and how marketisation has taken hold of the HE sector in England and elsewhere?

NEOLIBERALISM

According to Birch (2015, p. 572), there is consensus that neoliberalism can be broadly defined "as the extension and installation of competitive markets into all areas of life, including the economy, politics, and society".

The market is arguably the central concept within neoliberalism, and market competition is seen as the mechanism for achieving possible outcomes for all within society. Competition is, therefore, the only legitimate organising principle for human activity (Metcalf, 2017). The neoliberal promotes and endorses the value of market competition under all circumstances, as it is seen as the most efficient and moral institution for organising human life. Neoliberalism treats competition as the crucial and most valuable feature of capitalism (Gane, 2020). Through the neutral market competition mechanism, we discover who and what is valuable rather than following a particular viewpoint imposed by politicians, philosophers, planners, or the outcomes of the political process. It also argues that "human well-being can best be advanced by liberating individual entrepreneurial freedoms and skills within an institutional framework characterised by strong property rights, free markets and free trade" (Harvey, 2006, p. 2). Likewise, the market is also the key mechanism to create and maintain social order as opposed to the family, society, and, most importantly, the state.

Neoliberalism has been a controversial concept for decades. Major points of contention relate to its meaning as well as its analytic value. Despite its continuing popularity, there is considerable ambiguity about what the term means, could mean, or should mean. The concept is undoubtedly interpreted, used, and arguably abused in many different ways, and therefore, it can mean many things (Mudge, 2008; Hardin, 2014). Boas and Gans-Morse (2009) found that within the academic literature, the term is often undefined, and it is used to characterise a wide range of phenomena. Others, including Peck (2008, 2010), maintained that, due to its complex history and its ascription of different meanings by rival groups of political economists, it remains an ambiguous concept and is impossible to reduce to a single essence. For Hall (2011), its usage is so broad that it has become reductive and unsatisfactory. Birch (2015, p. 573), for example, suggested that "when [neoliberalism] is used critically to mean almost anything bad or disagreeable from corporate power to rampant individualism, it can end up becoming nothing more than an anti-liberal slogan of little analytical use".

Related to the problems of ambiguity and misuse is concern about the conceptual value of neoliberalism. Some have questioned its value due to this lack of agreement on the value and its subsequent ubiquity in the literature (Flew, 2014; Gamble, 2001; Nonini, 2008; Rowlands & Rawolle, 2013). Others have taken issue with a perceived ideological and normative application (Barnett, 2009) and even perceived it as conspiratory

(Venugopal, 2015). Its usage tends to be disproportionally mobilised and deployed by critical observers, overwhelmingly left-wing academics and activists (Larner, 2006, p. 450). According to Dean (2014, 150), neoliberalism is a rather overblown notion that "has been used, usually by a certain kind of critic, to characterise everything from a particular brand of free-market political philosophy and a wide variety of innovations in public management to patterns and processes found in and across diverse political spaces and territories around the globe". Others have argued that the theoretical concept is not reflected well in actual practice (Birch, 2015). It is also true that very few voices would identify with the label; therefore, it may represent more of an interpretation of a set of ideological changes than an actual mainstream political position. In the last decade, more and more scholars have raised the question of whether we have moved beyond neoliberalism (Davies & Gane, 2021; Peck & Theodore, 2019; Springer, 2014). Yet, despite these concerns, it is one of the most enduring concepts within the social sciences and continues to be used throughout the description of a wide range of developments and states.

Marketisation

What defines marketisation is the dominance of the market mechanism, as found in the free market. In an educational setting, education is obliged to be a marketplace that coordinates demand from market actors and suppliers (or providers). Market actors must choose freely based on individual choices. A marketised system can be upheld by policies that push educational institutions to act as market actors for which self-steering and accountability are needed (Jongbloed, 2003, p. 114).

Marketisation is expressed through key market principles that have permeated much of the HE system in England (Tholen, 2022, p. 5), as follows:

- pursuit of markets and competition between universities and courses
- private sector managerialism and rationalism in the governance of universities
- transferring the cost of HE to students
- student choice concept of customer–provider relationships in HE between students and institutions
- the drive for value for money of running HE towards students and the taxpayer.

Marketisation is often seen as a force damaging HE for various reasons (Brown, 2011, 2013; John & Fanghanel, 2016; Molesworth et al., 2010). Some have warned that marketisation reduces the public role that HE institutions play in society (De La Fuente, 2002; Heller, 2016). Market forces are turning university education into a commodified good, damaging its integrity and substance (Deem, 2001; Gibbs, 2001). Others argue that it corrodes the intrinsic value of higher learning and replaces it with an instrumental one (Collini, 2017). HE is seen as traditionally supporting the democratic and civic life of the nation, and marketisation is deteriorating this role (Daniels et al., 2021). Proponents of marketisation in HE are far fewer in number but offer arguments that it helps provide better value for its users, that is, students and the taxpayer. They see it as the most sensible route to running and financing mass HE, improving accountability and being more likely to aid economic development (Brown, 2011; Willetts, 2017).

It is hard to deny that the British HE system has moved in a market direction over time. Examples are that the criteria for university degrees have been liberalised, and the tuition fee has been raised to fully cover the cost of undergraduate teaching. The growing influence of university rankings and guides to quality has increased incentives for institutions to raise funds from private sources, growing managerialism, and increasing commodification. For many countries, a form of marketisation occurred alongside the growth of HE itself. Very few countries have stayed free from marketisation. Likewise, in no country has HE completely opened up to free market competition. This book focuses predominantly on the English context, which can be placed at the more marketised end of the spectrum. The English market for HE is not free or pure. As Brown (2013, p. 25) points out, a 'pure' market would have legally autonomous institutions, little or no regulation of market entry, and no regulatory limits on the prices charged (fees) or the numbers enrolled (among others). None of these apply in the English context. It is more helpful to think about how forms of market and competition have been inserted into the system, while non-market elements remain.

Marketisation as Neoliberalism

A key question is why marketisation has proliferated in the last 30 years. Also, why has it been advanced in some countries but not in others? Some have argued that it should be seen as a natural phenomenon primarily caused by political concerns about affordability for taxpayers (Palfreyman & Tapper, 2014). The funding for HE has been deliberately shifted towards the users, namely, the students, who then effectively become consumers of education. The provision of HE would then need to be coordinated by markets. For others, it is neoliberalism that is the culprit. Marketisation results from a force of change that affects all levels of education (Association of Colleges, 2020; Ball, 2003; Pratt, 2016), but HE is arguably the most important. Neoliberalism is reshaping the content and practice of HE both in education and research (e.g. Balan, 2023; Barnett, 2000; Brazzill, 2021; Ingleby, 2021; Giroux, 2010, 2014; Levidow, 2005; Lynch, 2006; Newfield, 2011; Olssen & Peters, 2005; Radice, 2015; Saunders, 2010, Schram, 2015; Smyth, 2017). Vernon (2018, p. 268) described the process of neoliberalism taking over US HE gradually and covertly, albeit all-encompassingly:

> It was not until the 1990s that the practices that slowly, and fitfully, remade the university in its current neoliberal forms were instantiated. […] a deeply messy, contingent, and uneven set of processes, set in motion by a variety of agents, discourses, and practices, gradually recast the university as a neoliberal institution. We can characterize these processes, following Andrew McGettigan, as those of marketization, privatization, and financialization. […] these practices sought to establish a new type of academic subject and an economized common sense about the purpose, management, and experience of higher education.

As mentioned earlier, in the literature, neoliberalism in HE drives a wide range of developments, including privatisation and commercialisation, the growth of capitalist and corporate influences over higher education institutions, privatisation, managerialism, consumerism, the role of private funding, and the elimination of the concepts of the public good or community, to be replaced with "individual responsibility" (Maisuria & Cole, 2017, p. 604).[1] Mintz (2021, pp. 81–82) likewise mentioned the following broad characteristics:

- the belief in the efficiency of the free market
- the need to deregulate the economy and privatise the public sector
- the commitment to tax reduction, the abandonment of the welfare state
- the replacement of the notion of the public good with personal responsibility for one's own welfare.

Almost invariably, the literature on neoliberalism and HE understands marketisation to be part of a neoliberal drive. The idea that neoliberalism caused marketisation is presumed to be a fact by education scholars and widely discussed in HE literature (e.g. Aranowitz, 2001; Lynch, 2006; Giroux & Giroux, 2004; Hill, 2003; Levidow, 2005; McLaren, 2005; Slaughter & Rhoades, 2004). The neoliberal agenda aims to transform public services into private goods, offloading the costs to individual users, and making HE another market commodity. Universities are "run purely as businesses" (Lynch, 2006, p. 1). Some see marketisation as an almost pure neoliberal phenomenon. Maisura and Cole (2017, p. 605) stated, "HE policy agenda is becoming more explicitly neoliberal, the enmeshing of neoliberalism in education over the last three decades has been so deep, intensive and all-encompassing it has become almost natural". Roger Brown (2018), a key scholar in the study of marketisation in HE, argued:

1 *Marketisation is the link between Neoliberalism and higher education: marketisation is how Neoliberalism reshapes the provision of higher education, as it does nearly every other social activity.*
2 *Marketisation has broadly the same impact on the provision of higher education as Neoliberalism has on society and the economy generally.*

Is It Really Neoliberalism?

Although there is a considerable consensus in the literature that neoliberalism is the culprit of marketisation or, at the least, has something to do with marketisation, we need to be critical about whether marketisation in HE is indeed caused, driven, or supported by neoliberalisation or part of a larger neoliberal takeover. Here, we need to fully assess whether the key tenets of marketisation are indeed congruous with the aim of neoliberal governance. We also look at the empirical evidence of how and why markets have been used in the organisation of HE. It may seem enticing to connect anything to do with competition, markets, or even instrumental rationales as neoliberal or part of the 'neoliberal university'. There is a risk that it comes as a catch-all concept used to sum up all that is wrong with HE. There is also a risk that the concept of neoliberalism would be rather meaningless analytically if we presume that the whole HE system embodies it. Likewise, our understanding of marketisation is compromised if we do not critically assess why and how neoliberalism relates to it or which parts it affects.

Others have gone before to scrutinise the extent to which modern universities can be called neoliberal. Dougherty and Natow (2020), for instance, examined how the concept of neoliberalism captures performance-based funding for HE. They identified various areas where the theory correctly predicts the impacts, origins, and implementation, but less so in other areas. For instance, according to the authors, neoliberal theory rightly anticipates the key role that top government officials play in the development of performance-based funding but not the role of business, HE institutions, inter-state actors, and policy networks. Both Watts (2017) and McCaig (2018) evaluate the concept of neoliberalism in relation to HE marketisation and offered insights into how neoliberalism can be applied to recent HE policies, including those stimulating the role of markets. However, their works do not aim to provide a detailed assessment. Given its popularity within the study of marketisation on HE, the topic warrants a more extensive and more focused in-depth analysis of neoliberalism, giving a more structured answer to the role of neoliberalism in HE marketisation.

Rationale of the Book

This book investigates whether neoliberalism is the driver of marketisation in HE. It aims to elucidate how the greater use of markets to manage and function HE can be attributed as a neoliberal phenomenon. This is a complex question for many reasons. One issue this book deals with is the multiple meanings of neoliberalism. How we understand neoliberalism will thus change the answer to the question of how neoliberalism is related to marketisation.

The book argues that the concept of neoliberalism to describe the direction HE is shifting towards is useful in many ways, but it is rather inadequate on its own. Imposing market rationality and consumer choice on HE follows a neoliberal rulebook. However, one of the problems that those who use the notion of the neoliberal concept face in explaining how and why marketisation has taken place is the lack of specificity regarding where the principle of neoliberalism applies. Also, rationales behind increasing marketisation have been wide-ranging, often created ad hoc, and not always caused by a strong ideological drive. The book aims to advance our current understanding of marketisation in HE by offering a detailed assessment of the key political motives and manifestations of marketisation, examining predominantly the education function of HE (as opposed to research).

The Organisation of the Book

The next chapter, Chap. 2, sets out the historical context within which the influence of neoliberalism on HE took place and offers a short history of HE in the English context. It describes how universities have always had multiple purposes, although, until the 1960s, the intrinsic non-economic aims of universities were heightened and accepted. After this, and especially from the 1980s onwards, the economic-instrumental aims of HE took the foreground, particularly in government thinking. The idea that the purpose of universities is to provide students with human capital and serve the economy more widely slowly became dominant.

Chapter 3 examines the concept of neoliberalism. It consists of two parts. The first part offers an intellectual history of key neoliberal thinkers and ideas. It covers the Austrian and Chicago Schools as well as proponents of public choice theory. The second part distinguishes three ways neoliberalism has been understood: a) as policy, b) as ideology, and c) as governmentality.

Chapter 4 explores how the concept of neoliberalism has been used in the academic literature on HE. It observes that for many in the field of education, neoliberalism is used to critique a range of processes and practices in and management of the HE sector or specifically (public) universities. The chapter then demonstrates how all three approaches of neoliberalism outlined in Chap. 3 can be applied to comprehend changes within HE and universities.

Chapter 5 is dedicated to the concept of marketisation in HE. Drawing on Chap. 4, it offers an assessment of the idea that neoliberalism is the driver of marketisation. The chapter differentiates five different areas: market, competition, finance, the state, and universities. For each of these, it will show that different approaches to neoliberalism fit these themes best.

Chapter 6 is the book's final chapter and looks back at how and to what extent the concept of neoliberalism can be used to understand marketisation in HE. It argues that there is scope to use the concept of neoliberalism, but it will not fit all areas. Also, at least three distinct approaches to neoliberalism can be used to understand, more specifically, the role of neoliberalism. This chapter reflects on what these arguments mean for our understanding of marketisation and neoliberalism. The chapter ends with an alternative framing of the role of neoliberalism in HE, which draws on wider changes in society's understanding of what universities are for.

Note

1. Some seemingly find any market-related changes to be neoliberal (e.g. Schraedley et al., 2021; del Cerro Santamaría, 2020).

References

Aranowitz, S. (2001). *The Knowledge Factory: Dismantling the Corporate University and Creating True Higher Learning*. Beacon Press.
Association of Colleges. (2020). *The Impact of Competition in Post-16 Education & Training*. AoC.
Balan, A. (2023). Neoliberalism, privatisation and marketisation: The implications for legal education in England and Wales. *Cogent Education, 10*(2).
Ball, S. J. (2003). The teacher's soul and the terrors of performativity. *Journal of Education Policy, 18*(2), 215–228.
Ball, S. J. (2015). Living the neo-liberal university. *European Journal of Education, 50*(3), 258–261.
Barnett, R. (2000). *Realising the University in an Age of Supercomplexity*. Open University Press.
Barnett, C. (2009). Publics and markets: What's wrong with neoliberalism? In S. Smith, R. Pain, S. Marston, & J. P. Jones (Eds.), *The Sage Handbook of Social Geography* (pp. 269–296). Sage.
Birch, K. (2015). Neoliberalism: The whys and wherefores … and future directions. *Sociology Compass, 9*(7), 571–584.
Boas, T. C., & Gans-Morse, J. (2009). Neoliberalism: From new liberal philosophy to anti-liberal slogan. *Studies in Comparative International Development, 44*(2), 137–161.
Brazzill, M. (2021). The development of higher education in Japan and the United Kingdom: The impact of neoliberalism. *Higher Education Quarterly, 75*(3), 381–397.
Brown, R. (2011a). Introduction. In R. Brown (Ed.), *Higher Education and the Market* (pp. 1–6). Routledge.
Brown, R. (2011b). *Higher Education and the Market*. Routledge.
Brown, R. (2013). *Everything for Sale? The Marketization of UK Higher Education*. Routledge.

Brown, R. (2018). *Neoliberalism, Marketisation and Higher Education*. Speech Edge Hill University, June 14. Retrieved April 22, 2024, from https://www.youtube.com/watch?v=pMpiiVxNd8g

Collini, S. (2017). *Speaking of Universities*. Verso Books.

Daniels, R. J., Shreve, G., & Spector, P. (2021). *What Universities Owe Democracy*. John Hopkins University Press.

Davies, W., & Gane, N. (2021). Post-Neoliberalism? An introduction. *Theory, Culture & Society, 38*(6), 3–28.

De La Fuente, J. R. (2002). Academic freedom and social responsibility. *Higher Education Policy, 15*(4), 337–339.

Dean, M. (2014). Rethinking neoliberalism. *Journal of Sociology, 50*(2), 150–163.

Deem, R. (2001). Globalisation, new managerialism, academic capitalism and entrepreneurialism in universities: Is the local dimension still important? *Comparative Education, 37*(1), 7–20.

Del Cerro Santamaría, G. D. (2020). Challenges and drawbacks in the marketisation of higher education within neoliberalism. *Review of European Studies, 12*(1), 22–38.

Dougherty, K. J., & Natow, R. S. (2020). Performance-based funding for higher education: How well does neoliberal theory capture neoliberal practice? *Higher Education, 80*(3), 457–478.

Flew, T. (2014). Six theories of neoliberalism. *Thesis Eleven, 122*(1), 49–71.

Foskett, N. (2011). Markets, government, funding and the marketisation of higher education. In M. Molesworth, R. Scullion, & E. Nixon (Eds.), *The Marketisation of Higher Education and the Student* (pp. 25–38). Routledge.

Gamble, A. (2001). Neo-liberalism. *Capital and Class, 25*(1), 127–134.

Gane, N. (2020). Competition: A critical history of a concept. *Theory, Culture & Society, 37*(2), 31–59.

Gerrard, J. (2015). Public education in neoliberal times: Memory and desire. *Journal of Education Policy, 30*(6), 855–868.

Gibbs, P. (2001). Higher education as a market: A problem or solution? *Studies in Higher Education, 26*(1), 85–94.

Giroux, H. A. (2010). Bare pedagogy and the scourge of neoliberalism: Rethinking higher education as a democratic public sphere. *The Educational Forum, 74*(3), 184–196.

Giroux, H. A. (2014). *Neoliberalism's War on Higher Education*. Haymarket Books.

Giroux, H. A., & Giroux, S. S. (2004). *Take Back Higher Education*. Palgrave Macmillan.

Hall, S. (2011). The neoliberal revolution. *Soundings, 48*, 9–28.

Hardin, C. (2014). Finding the 'Neo' in neoliberalism. *Cultural Studies, 28*(2), 199–221.

Harvey, D. (2006). *A Brief History of Neoliberalism*. Oxford University Press.

Heller, H. (2016). *The Capitalist University: The Transformations of Higher Education in the United States since 1945*. Pluto Press.
Hill, D. (2003). Global neo-liberalism, the deformation of education and resistance. *The Journal for Critical Education Policy Studies., 1*(1), 1–50.
Hill, D., & Kumar, R. (Eds.). (2011). *Global Neoliberalism and Education and its Consequences*. Routledge.
Holmwood, J. (Ed.). (2011). *A Manifesto for the Public University*. Bloomsbury. https://www.theguardian.com/news/2017/aug/18/neoliberalism-the-idea-that-changed-the-world
Ingleby, E. (2021). *Neoliberalism Across Education: Policy and Practice from Early Childhood Through Adult Learning*. Palgrave Macmillan.
John, P., & Fanghanel, J. (Eds.). (2016). *Dimensions of Marketisation in Higher Education*. Routledge.
Jones, B. M. A., & Ball, S. J. (2023). *Neoliberalism and Education*. Routledge.
Jongbloed, B. (2003). Marketisation in higher education, Clark's triangle and the essential ingredients of markets. *Higher Education Quarterly, 57*(2), 110–135.
Larner, W. (2006). Review of a brief history of neoliberalism. *Economic Geography, 82*, 449–451.
Levidow, L. (2005). Neoliberal agendas for higher education. In A. Saad-Filho & D. Johnston (Eds.), *Neoliberalism: A Critical Reader* (pp. 156–163). Pluto Press.
Lynch, K. (2006). Neo-liberalism land Marketisation: The implications for Higher Education. *European Educational Research Journal, 5*(1), 1–17.
Maisuria, A. (2014). The neo-liberalisation policy agenda and its consequences for education in England: A focus on resistance now and possibilities for the future. *Policy Futures in Education, 12*(2), 286–296.
Maisuria, A., & Cole, M. (2017). The neoliberalization of higher education in England: An alternative is possible. *Policy Futures in Education, 15*(5), 602–619.
McCaig, C. (2018). *The Marketisation of English Higher Education: A Policy Analysis of a Risk-based System*. Emerald.
McGettigan, A. (2013). *The Great University Gamble: Money, Markets and the Future of Higher Education*. Pluto Press.
McLaren, P. (2005). *Capitalist and Conquerors: A Critical Pedagogy against Empire*. Rowman & Littlefield.
Metcalf, S. (2017). Neoliberalism: The idea that swallowed the world. *The Guardian*, August 18. Retrieved April 22, 2024, from https://www.theguardian.com/news/2017/aug/18/neoliberalism-the-idea-that-changed-the-world
Mintz, B. (2021). Neoliberalism and the crisis in higher education: The cost of ideology. *American Journal of Economics and Sociology, 80*(1), 79–112.
Molesworth, M., Scullion, R., & Nixon, E. (Eds.). (2010). *The Marketisation of Higher Education: The Student as Consumer*. Routledge.

Mudge, S. L. (2008). The state of the art: What is neo-liberalism? *Socio-Economic Review, 6*, 703–731.
Newfield, C. (2011). *Unmaking the Public University: The Forty-Year Assault on the Middle Class*. Harvard University Press.
Nonini, D. (2008). Is China becoming neoliberal? *Critique of Anthropology, 28*(2), 145–176.
Olssen, M., & Peters, M. A. (2005). Neoliberalism, higher education and the knowledge economy: From the free market to knowledge capitalism. *Journal of Education Policy, 20*(3), 313–345.
Palfreyman, D., Tapper, T., & T. (2014). *Reshaping the University: The Rise of the Regulated Market in Higher Education*. Oxford University Press.
Peck, J. (2008). Remaking laissez-faire. *Progress in Human Geography, 32*(1), 3–43.
Peck, J. (2010). *Constructions of Neoliberal Reason*. Oxford University Press.
Peck, J., & Theodore, N. (2019). Still neoliberalism? *South Atlantic Quarterly, 118*(2), 245–265.
Pratt, N. (2016). Neoliberalism and the (internal) marketisation of primary school assessment in England. *British Educational Research Journal, 42*(5), 890–905.
Radice, H. (2015). How we got here: UK higher education under neoliberalism. *ACME: An International Journal for Critical Geographies, 12*(2), 407–418.
Rowlands, J., Rawolle, S., & S. (2013). Neoliberalism is not a theory of everything: A Bourdieuian analysis of illusio in educational research. *Critical Studies in Education, 54*(3), 260–272.
Saunders, D. B. (2010). Neoliberal ideology and public higher education in the United States. *Journal for Critical Education Policy Studies, 8*(1), 41–77.
Schraedley, M. A., Jenkins, J. J., Irelan, M., & Umana, M. (2021). The neoliberalization of higher education: Paradoxing students' basic needs at a hispanic-serving institution. *Frontiers in Sustainable Food Systems, 5*(689499), 1–13.
Schram, S. (2015). *The Return of Ordinary Capitalism: Neoliberalism, Precarity, Occupy*. Oxford University Press.
Slaughter, S., & Rhoades, G. (2004). *Academic Capitalism and the New Economy: Markets, State and Higher Education*. Johns Hopkins University Press.
Smyth, J. (2017). *The Toxic University: Zombie Leadership, Academic Rock Stars, and Neoliberal Ideology*. Palgrave Macmillan.
Springer, S. (2014). Postneoliberalism? *Review of Radical Political Economics, 47*(1), 5–17.
Tett, L., & Hamilton, M. (Eds.). (2021). *Resisting Neoliberalism in Education: Local, National and Transnational Perspectives*. Policy Press.
Tholen, G. (2022). *Modern Work and the Marketisation of Higher Education*. Policy Press.
Venugopal, R. (2015). Neoliberalism as concept. *Economy and Society, 44*(2), 165–187.

Vernon, J. (2018). The making of the neoliberal university in Britain. *Critical Historical Studies, 5*(2), 267-280.
Watts, R. (2017). *Public Universities, Managerialism and the Value of Higher Education*. Palgrave Macmillan.
Willetts, D. (2017). *A University Education*. Oxford University Press.
Williams, G. (2004). The higher education market in the United Kingdom. In P. Teixeira, B. Jongbloed, D. Dill, & A. Amaral (Eds.), *Markets in Higer Education: Rhetoric or Reality?* (pp. 241–269). Springer.

CHAPTER 2

HE in Flux

Abstract This chapter describes the historical context in which the influence of neoliberalism on HE took place, offering a succinct history of higher education in the English context. It explains how universities have always had multiple purposes, yet, until the 1960s, the intrinsic non-economic aims of universities were heightened and accepted. After this, and especially from the 1980s onwards, the economic-instrumental aims of HE were foregrounded, particularly in government thinking. The idea that the purpose of universities is to provide students with human capital and serve the economy more widely slowly became dominant.

Keywords Universities • Purpose • Instrumentalism • History

> *Future historians, pondering changes in British society from the 1980s onwards, will struggle to account for the following curious fact. Although British business enterprises have an extremely mixed record (frequently posting gigantic losses, mostly failing to match overseas competitors, scarcely benefiting the weaker groups in society), and although such arm's length public institutions as museums and galleries, the BBC and the universities have by and large a very good record (universally acknowledged creativity, streets ahead of most of their international peers, positive forces for human development and social cohesion),*

> nonetheless over the past three decades politicians have repeatedly attempted to force the second set of institutions to change so that they more closely resemble the first. Some of those historians may even wonder why at the time there was so little concerted protest at this deeply implausible programme. (Collini, 2013, p. 12)

This chapter offers the historical and intellectual context in which marketisation in HE has taken place. It outlines a brief historical overview of how HE, particularly universities, has been understood. It explores the lineage of thought about the purpose and organisation of HE, including foundational texts that established the idea of the university far before neoliberalism emerged. How we define a situation shapes how we act upon it. The way we define HE informs what we believe is possible and desirable. The need for marketisation makes sense once you accept the perceived role of HE in society. By exploring how we think about the role of HE in society, we can better understand the appropriate place of the market mechanism. As such, the chapter maps a history of ideas regarding the role of HE and how HE should be organised to fulfil these aims. The chapter covers some influential scholars, such as Wilhelm von Humboldt and Cardinal John Henry Newman, who helped to articulate some of the university's perceived key characteristics: the autonomy of the institution, academic freedom, critical thinking, the balance of teaching and research, and liberal education. The chapter also identifies a shift in what HE ought to do, moving to more instrumental and economic aims.

The analysis is here concise, and more in-depth and detailed examinations of the history of HE have been written (e.g. Anderson, 2006; Lowe, 2008). The purpose of this short history of ideas on universities is to provide a foundation (or framework) upon which neoliberal influence on HE can be explained and evaluated. It will try to explain how marketisation is entwined with the decline in the ideal of the university that dominated for various centuries in the British context. The perceived aims and purposes of HE made further marketisation possible. The influence of markets within English HE has been a slow process that accelerated noticeably from the 1980s onwards. So for the longest time, marketisation was not the dominant force, but of course, HE has never been free of competition, and universities have been part of a market for education in various forms since the early days. However, our understanding of the role and aim of universities has shifted partly because of political ideas around the role of market and competition and HE management. An overview of key ideas around the purpose of HE is of use to clarify and contextualise the influence of neoliberalism and to help explain its role. How has marketisation taken hold of an institution that was traditionally largely protected from it?

The purposes of HE, and universities specifically, have always been multiple. They were also open to interpretation and have changed over time. They include transmitting a body of knowledge for the core professions, fostering scientific enquiry for furthering the interests of the nation-state, serving diverse societal interests—community, industry, government—and driving economic growth through human capital formation and technological innovation. As Rothblatt (1997, p. 1) stressed, "A single idea of a university has never truly existed [...] In approximately 800 years of history, the university as an institution has served many different cultures and societies". Also, HE has always had multiple competing or complementary rationales, most prominently religious goals, nation-state building, and answering the political and industrial revolutions. Differentiation in its forms and roles but also of its curriculum (see Clark, 2006) has been a key characteristic of HE in the UK and elsewhere (Carpentier, 2018). Throughout its history, new types of HE institutions emerged, and old ones were transformed or disappeared altogether. The idea of the university is not set in stone and is ongoing (Peters & Barnett, 2018, p. 14). Yet, there is a canon that can be identified, and it is clear that it has changed over time and is potentially affected by what we could call neoliberalism. This chapter outlines a simplified intellectual lineage of ideas about what universities should be occupied with, in particular focusing on education. We can map the rise and fall of the intrinsic and non-economic aims of HE that stand in contrast to a sense of purpose supported by instrumental and economic objectives.

Early Ideas

The historical origins of universities as key institutions in HE have been well documented (Pedersen, 1998; de Ridder-Symoens, 1992). In various cities in Europe, places of learning emerged from the twelfth century onwards as self-governing institutions that came to resemble what we call universities today. According to Willetts (2017, p. 14), what historically defines the university is its status as a self-governing independent corporation. Early universities tended to have a wide curriculum and some specific focus on theology, law, or medicine. They were closely aligned with the church, the state, and key professions, producing and transmitting knowledge and effectively providing higher technical education (theology, law, and medicine) (Carpentier, 2015). Universities became central societal institutions, often part of growing political and religious battles. They also became a strategic asset within medieval Europe. Early European states made the political aspect of universities even more pronounced and played an important role in the construction of national and religious identity (Carpentier, 2019). Over time, universities have become not merely sites of scholarship and the development of interpretations of existing knowledge, but also centres of research.

Various waves of expansion increased the number of universities and institutions. Their professional preparation was mainly in service of the church and civil law; however, there was an indirect influence through university-educated leaders within many other professions (O'Day, 2009). In the English context, the universities of Oxford and Cambridge had a monopoly on HE until 1828, when University College London opened. Their approach to teaching excluded non-Anglicans and strongly served the formation of elites. Rustin (2016) reminds us:

> Until the nineteenth century, their principal function was more to provide a cultural and social formation for elites than to produce useful knowledge. (The Royal Society, and provincial societies and networks, and not the universities, were the early incubators of the scientific and technological revolution in England—Scotland had a different tradition.) We can thus see the original role of English universities as one of cultural reproduction and transmission for a predominantly aristocratic social fraction, which did however offer some opportunities for social mobility for talented individuals from lower classes, and gave capabilities to the state and the church.

Oxford and Cambridge were instrumental and vocational (Anderson, 2006), but independent from both ecclesiastical and state control. As a mechanism, the credentialing process emerged to assure society that only those with approved qualifications would be allowed to practise a particular occupation. In Europe, a new demand for more secular, professional, and scientific education driven by the Enlightenment led to expansion, differentiation, and professionalisation. Carpentier (2019) observed that a characteristic of the early modern era is the emergence of a new social rationale for HE. This may have been linked to elitism, as suggested by changes in enrolment. Institutions became more aristocratic, preoccupied with the new social function of educating the elites.

Nineteenth Century

We fast forward to the nineteenth century when the contours of the contemporary university became apparent. Collini (2012) reminds us that the modern university is very much a nineteenth-century creation. For instance, until then, there was no expectation that a university would be engaged in both teaching and research (Evans, 2018). These establishments became centres of higher learning rather than merely vocationally oriented schools. Research was becoming one of the defining features of the university. In addition, the needs of the economy started to transform universities and energised other forms of HE. New university colleges and civic universities that emerged took a similar secular and utilitarian approach. Newly founded universities took on a new purpose, geared towards scientific discovery and, particularly, the incorporation of engineering linked to industrial needs (Sanderson, 1972). Their creation also responded to the growing demand of the middle classes, which were looking for improved social status and advanced technical education.

A key influence on how nineteenth-century universities developed is the work of Wilhelm von Humboldt (1767–1835). The 'Humboldtian' university became a model for the other European (especially German) and US universities. It can be seen as the characteristic form of the university idea until the growth of mass HE in the late twentieth century. The reforms of Wilhelm von Humboldt in Prussia came with a strong notion of an idea of the university, particularly the idea that the university should include research and teaching. He argued for the union of teaching and research in the role of the scholar, and research becoming an integral part of every university's activities. Humboldt became a strong advocate for institutional autonomy and the academic freedom of scholars, even in a system where universities were under the direct control of the state. The state should not directly intervene in the universities and was not to make demands on the universities. Humboldt also stressed a long humanist tradition that ties university education to broader emancipation and human development goals.

A dominant idea that has shaped HE until this day is the idea that university education should play a key role in people's individual growth, such as self-formation or self-realisation, also known as the *Bildung view*. The German word 'Bildung', often translated as self-formation or self-realisation, the idea that education can aid human self-perfection, became enmeshed in these ideas (Lovlie & Standish, 2003). By refining and completing oneself as a human being, a university education draws students' capability to grasp the unity of knowledge that drives individual creative potential, which has ethical and political implications. Through Bildung, individuals have reached and internalised the highest values of national culture. As such, it makes it possible to claim civil and political rights. Universities should be designed to explore inner humanity as well as one's position in the world. Von Humboldt, one of the key thinkers associated with this ideal, emphasised that personality development is aimed at cultivating genuine individuality and should be central to a student's education. Education becomes an individualised spiritual and cultural experience that creates personal expansion and growth, providing society with well-informed human beings and citizens. It would serve only as a basis for subsequent vocational or professional training to be provided mainly in the workplace. Cultivation of the mind and character is supplemented with the acquisition of knowledge through participation in the research process. The university becomes an autonomous academic space ruled by free and equal faculty members. King (2003) observed that around the 1850s, liberal education was largely free of utility and vocationalism. Universities aimed to disseminate and advance original and critical knowledge to the benefit of society "not just to transmit the legacy of the past or to teach skills" (Anderson, 2010).

The German concept of Bildung did not penetrate very deeply into British universities until the end of the nineteenth century. Of great significant influence was Cardinal John Henry Newman's classic book *The Idea of a University* (1996), which broadly supported the Bildung view (with some more emphasis on the cultivation of the mind). His thoughts on what students should learn at university were equally compelling. Newman argued that universities, as modern places of learning, should teach universal knowledge and avoid a utilitarian or vocational approach to learning. His emphasis on teaching that encompasses all branches of knowledge, including theology, reveals a plea for liberal education. Rather than specialising in a field, students need to make connections between intellectual fields to truly understand the unity of knowledge. Newman thought that knowledge should be pursued 'for its own sake'. But by this, he did not mean pure research. For him, the search for truth was part of an educational ideal that shaped the cultivated man's personality and was inseparable from moral and religious education. This ideal required a pastoral relationship between teacher and student, and it derived from Newman's early experience as a college tutor at Oxford. The teaching function of universities drives many of Newman's arguments and his ideal of a liberal education. Students are not merely taught in their discipline but are immersed in a wider range of sciences to cultivate the student's inner life and educate global citizens (Nussbaum, 1997). Newman's ideas have persisted and still impact our thinking about what universities should be (Edwards, 2004, p. 30).

The growth of English universities in the nineteenth century was significant and supported by the rise of the national state and the need for national self-knowledge rooted in the search for truth and a kind of virtue and spiritual vocation (Peters & Barnett, 2018, p. 21). The state also had a clear interest in science and technology as part of economic nationalist strategy. In the second half of the nineteenth century, England saw the rise of professional education and civic education (King, 2003). Universities in England had multiplied with the founding of new universities in the growing industrial cities, and the question of the practical usefulness of a degree was beginning to exert pressure. These civic universities came along in the 1890s and 1900s as the work of the local elites' expression of civic pride in industrial and trading cities such as Birmingham, Leeds, Liverpool, Manchester, and Sheffield, supporting mining, brewing, textiles, and chemical industries (Palleyfrey & Tapper, 2014, p. 70). The links with industry intensified throughout the twentieth century and started to be conceived as inextricably tight. The modern universities in the early modern period continued to focus on developing industrial skills that could be acquired by formal education (and in some cases concentrated exclusively on technical education). The new universities' vocational and industrial focus in the nineteenth century did not diminish the intrinsic and non-instrumental values attached to universities.

It is true that, ultimately, most new universities in the nineteenth century developed a more pragmatic route than Newman had envisioned. Inspired by the Oxford model, he disapproved of the newer conceptions of universities. Whereas Newman stressed the importance of teaching, research became a key role of universities. Newer civic-oriented universities also needed to teach subjects for which they could recruit. As Rothblatt argued, "They were, to begin with, market-driven, fee-sensitive, vulnerable to changes in demand and willing to take students with weaker preparation than mid-Victorian Oxford and Cambridge" (Rothblatt, 1997, p. 21). Yet Newman's insistence that what needed to be taught should be according to students' own curiosity and the wide choice in subjects remained a key feature of the British universities and was even more important in the American system. This subsequently may also have affected the labour market transitions of graduates vis-à-vis those in European countries. In Britain, the idea that education should aim at producing generalists rather than narrow specialists remained strong. There was much value in non-vocational subjects, which could train the mind in ways that apply to various types of work. The development of character was especially important in elite universities in England and liberal arts colleges in the United States (Perkin, 2007).

After WW2, a distinct intellectual tradition remained, drawing on the Humboldtian and Newmanian theoretical foundations. Although these traditions have substantial differences, there is an agreement that the public and developmental role should prevail, as there is a growing demand for specific, vocational, or utilitarian forms of HE. Intellectuals, such as philosopher Karl Jaspers, emphasised the fundamental role HE has to play in the formation of the mind and wrote how the university is designed to arrive at truth and seek relations to the totality of all there is to be known. Jaspers expressed fear of HE institutions becoming specialised scientific technical institutions (Jaspers, 1961). Likewise, Jurgen Habermas also attached the need for Bildung to university education throughout his life (Habermas, 1987a, 1987b; see also Sørensen, 2015). He applies Bildung to a much wider societal need that can take place in the political public sphere (through the means of collective communication). Habermas's writing on universities acknowledges the need for the transmission of "technically-exploitable knowledge", but also its dominance leading to the emergence of the technical-rational university, which can overshadow the other roles that the university has (Habermas, 1987).

The Non-instrumental Aim of Universities

There exists a much wider canon of literature which argues for the public and non-instrumental purpose of university education than offered here (see Peters and Barnett (2018) for a historical overview). Collini (2017) observes that this idea of the university was highly influential in the nineteenth and twentieth centuries. University education was understood to be founded based on 'reason and enlightenment' and the search for impartial truth. According to this view, institutions should be driven by intellectual freedom under far-reaching autonomy, reaching for "the acquisition and making of knowledge for its own sake and not for the sake of the money which may be gained by knowing how to do certain things"

(Rothblatt, 1997, p. 17). This particular role of universities draws primarily on an intrinsic view of HE, which regards HE as valuable in itself; its value is expressed in the following ways:

- non-economic purposes to improve society
- the development of citizenship through emancipation
- personal development
- knowledge for the sake of knowledge

The intrinsic value of the university also reflects the elite status of universities' 'learned' professions—law, medicine, and the church—"to which 'liberal' education gave a distinctive ethos of service and social responsibility" (Anderson, 2010). This ideal of public service was a major driving force for HE well into the 1980s in most countries (Williams, 2013, p. 60) The non-economic intrinsic view has long been a dominant analytical and normative framework within higher education, yet with the emergence of mass higher education came a change in how university education was understood. The role of the state in financing HE is of significance here. Not until the late 1940s did grants from the Universities Grant Committee (UGC) become a significant part of university income (Shattock, 2008, 2013). Increases in public spending on HE and the growth in the number of university places became political aims which over time informed a more instrumental understanding of HE. In the UK context, the Robbins Report (hereafter, Report) in particular was an important turning point in the state's influence within the debate about what Universities were for.

EDUCATIONAL SHIFT: ROBBINS AND THE 1960S

In the early 1960s, university education still reached only 4% to 5% of the age group and led chiefly to the professions or public services. At that time, research conducted by universities was already fundamental in industry, the military, and the welfare state. In 1963, a report of the Committee on Higher Education commissioned by the British government and chaired by Lord Robbins, a professor at the London School of Economics, was published (Robbins, 1963). The Report emerged as a response to economic pressures as well as a political drive towards increasing social equality. Growing demand for HE urged policymakers to reshape HE (Shattock, 2012, pp. 134–136). The dream of a larger and fairer HE was becoming increasingly difficult for growing numbers of people with two or more A-levels, considered the minimum entrance qualification at that time. The Report famously advocated an increase in the number of available HE university places and partly as a result, HE expanded significantly.[1] For the first time, the "ability to benefit" was the guiding principle for HE participation. University places "should be available to all who were qualified for them by ability and attainment" (Robbins, 1963, para 30). Robbins's objective was to double the student population, which was achieved in 1972. All British universities (including Oxford and Cambridge) were incorporated into a single system. All undergraduate degree programmes were provided with the same funding regardless of institution, with variation only for higher-cost subjects, such as science, technology, engineering, and mathematics (STEM) STEM subjects. A national student support system was also established.

At the time of the Robbins Report, students were overwhelmingly drawn from the middle and upper classes. University degrees provided vocational training for high-status occupations in law, medicine, and engineering, so university education played an important role in the reproduction of privilege within society and the labour market. However, social change altered the societal perception of the role of HE. Increasingly, politicians thought that economic competitiveness depended on increases in knowledge in the workforce at large and on the contributions of research and the development of new technologies during the Cold War, which certainly highlighted the importance of technology within global competition.

ROBBINS: INTRINSIC OR INSTRUMENTAL?

The view of HE put forward by Robbins largely still highlighted its intrinsic value. Although it seemed to accept that HE had a clear role to play in the economy, for Robbins, HE was a public good as well as a right for able individuals to enjoy for a wider variety of reasons, many of which were non-economic. Holmwood (2014, p. 9) stated that the Robbins Report supports the civic role of universities:

> The axiom that higher education should be available to all who are qualified by ability and attainment is a clear endorsement of a social democratic view of education, as, indeed, is the emphasis upon the public benefit of

education as the cultivation of the mind and the role of higher education in facilitating cultural and democratic participation. Taken together, they entail the recognition that liberal economic, civil, and political rights require an underpinning of social rights to ensure their realization for all citizens.

HE was regarded as so important a public good as to require a full financial subsidy for all students engaged in it. Interestingly, the Report demonstrated a balance in what HE was supposed to be for. The Report identified four aims, or public benefits, that warrant public HE. These are the public benefit of a skilled and educated workforce (Robbins, 1963, para 25), the public benefit of HE in producing cultivated men and women (Robbins, 1963, para 26), the public benefit of securing the advancement of learning through the combination of teaching and research within institutions (Robbins, 1963, para 27), and the public benefit of providing a common culture and standards of citizenship (Robbins, 1963, para 28).

The Report commented that "The system as a whole must be judged deficient unless it provides adequately for all of them" (Robbins, 1963, para 29). Although there are areas in the Report that moved away from earlier conceptions of the university, for Robbins, economic imperatives were the focus of only one of four 'social ends' to which HE might be directed (1963, para 6). HE was also positioned as a vehicle for social mobility, creating improved economic opportunities. In the Report, the authors were clear that the role of the state should have clear limits and not intervene in, for instance, the design of curricula, the setting of standards, and the admission of students, nor should it control any public funding meant for universities (Evans, 2018, p. 78).

For Robbins, the essential aim of a first degree should be to teach the student how to think. Kelly et al. (2017, p. 107) highlighted the strong ideal of the student as a "cultivated person who would strive to understand, contemplate, and create the democratic conditions that enabled a set of shared social and cultural ideals to be realised" within the Report, as well as an outward collective pursuit of the good society. However, the Report also explicitly recognised the link between HE and the labour market (through private returns to the individual learner) and the UK economy. In addition, the idea that the demand from suitable candidates should determine the supply of HE places may have moved the needle towards marketisation.

After Robbins

After the 1960s, many new English universities and polytechnics were created, and participation rates for under-21s peaked at almost 14% in the 1970s before staying around that figure until the late 1980s (Mayhew et al., 2004). A constraint on public expenditure started in the mid-1970s when Britain's economy faced difficulties (Scott, 2021, p. 43). In his Ruskin College speech in 1976, Prime Minister James Callaghan urged educational institutions to meet the needs of employers in order to put his modernising mission into practice. Under the Conservative governments of 1979–1997, universities were further massified and more marketised. The Thatcher government radically transformed the British state and economy. There was a political desire to reduce the size and power of the public sector. Public services needed to be accountable for the funding they received and managed and to be more responsive to the needs of their users, who became more akin to 'customers' or 'consumers'. Thatcher reduced the budget of universities and introduced various market-oriented policy changes in the 1988 Education Reform Act. Markets and competition were at the heart of a new educational system. This included the business influence in the national curriculum and the governance and financing of schools (Fitz & Hafid, 2007) but also by promoting parental choice through the introduction of grant-maintained schools, funding linked to pupil numbers, and creating transparency in the educational achievement of schools. It took control of higher and further education provisions outside of local authority control, and from that point onwards, governments have controlled HE and intervened more actively while reducing the autonomy of HE institutions.

The Thatcher government heralded a fundamental change in the institutional self-governance of universities (Shattock, 2012, p. 220). They were treated as suppliers of services under contract with the state and other purchasers of their services. Contractual agreements between the new funding councils and universities were made based on the number of students recruited and the evaluation of the research produced, which drove increased competition between institutions and the rapid expansion of student numbers. During this time, a corporate management approach in running universities could be observed, driven by a greater perceived need for value for money and efficiency (especially after the 1985 Jarratt Report). Public-sector trade unions and academics were not often involved in decision making and lost power. Reforms saw greater demands on universities to increase their productivity, reduce their operating costs, improve their drop-out rates, and match the demands of the job market (Ferlie et al., 2009). According to Shattock (2012), the early 1980s represented a shift from the outside to inside model marks and a sea change in HE policies as they were no longer conceived and implemented by the university system but created outside the university system (Shattock, 2012, p. 7).

The Educational Reform Act of 1992 passed by John Major's government transferred control over polytechnics, which became 'new universities', from elected local councils to governing bodies. The latter consisted of governors drawn largely from business circles who had "little knowledge of HE, and tended to adopt a corporate model of what a university should be, for example in their approach to 'human resources', 'customer satisfaction', and financial priorities" (Rustin, 2016, p. 156). The expansion of new universities stretched the definition of what universities traditionally taught, with the inclusion of institutions that offered mainly practical and vocational courses delivered by staff who were not necessarily involved in research. As Lambert (2019) observed, "The power to award degrees, a right that had been rigorously guarded for decades, was handed out overnight".

The *1991 White Paper* (DES, 1991) is clear about the need for greater market reforms when it states, "[T]he Government believes that the real key to achieving cost-effective expansion lies in greater competition for funds and students. That can best be achieved by breaking down the increasingly artificial and unhelpful barriers between universities, polytechnics, and colleges" (DES, 1991, para 17). HE was increasingly seen as a consumption good, and universities were increasingly framed as service providers whose success was driven by efficient productivity and greater market demand. As publicly funded institutions, they were not seen as deserving of the autonomy they once enjoyed.

New Labour

The New Labour years were, in many ways, a continuation of the road the conservatives had travelled (Driver & Martell, 2006) yet with a new ideological positioning, creating HE policy along the same lines as their Third Way policies. Blair sought to combine social justice with economic prosperity, seeking to decrease inequality by giving those from deprived backgrounds access to HE to realise their talents within an economy that has become more fluid and open. Equality of opportunity became the dominant theme of Labour's economic policy, as well as its social policy. New Labour's modernisation of public services strengthened the model of consumption and 'consumers' of HE, and control over the universities also continued. Coates (2016, p. 74) observed:

> As governments struggled to explain and justify the expenditure of vast sums on universities (to themselves and the voters as much as anyone else), they realized the potential value of evaluation and performance measures. When Margaret Thatcher introduced such intrusive systems in the United Kingdom, they were tolerated, but barely, as short-term anomalies. But as subsequent governments revised and expanded oversight measures, it became clear that the evaluation revolution would not end soon.

Education policy was still driven by the assumption that parents would reward the best providers through choice (Clarke et al., 2007; Greener, 2008). The creation of league tables, together with a pupil-based funding formula, would improve standards (Bradley et al., 2004). There was a strong focus on providing better information to make informed choices, as poor user information was deemed a barrier to effective choices (Le Grand, 2007). HE became increasingly a market commodity fuelled by consumer demand (Tomlinson, 2001; Lunt, 2008; Whitty, 2009) and of greater importance than ever before for the competitiveness of the country in the global marketplace (Tholen, 2014). The perceived need to respond to a competitive global economy was coupled with a belief in the link between the economy and the knowledge and skills of the labour force and the 'commodification' of knowledge. The belief that a knowledge-based economy requires more and more highly qualified employees endorsed a continued commitment to increasing the total number of students and, within that, the overall proportion of graduate students. The requirement that Britain's HE should compete and stand among the top world-class universities meant a focus on further developing the research capacity and output of universities. According to New Labour thinking, globalisation reduces the proportion of low-skilled jobs as the role of manufacturing in the economy declines (Brown & Lauder, 2001). Education becomes of greater importance than ever before for the competitiveness of the country while at the same time promoting social mobility for those from disadvantaged backgrounds investing in higher advanced skills subject to global demand.

In 1997, the Dearing Report titled *Higher Education in the Learning Society* (NCIHE, 1997) made 93 recommendations on the future of HE. A key message was that students themselves should contribute to the cost of their tuition. All full-time undergraduates should contribute £1,000 per year of study after graduation on an income-contingent basis. Individual students (who were the beneficiaries of university education) should meet part of the costs of full-time HE when they could afford to. The introduction of fees was seen as needed to keep up with the growing demand for HE. The Dearing Report also argued for the expansion of student numbers and increased funding for research from the government.

The most important driver of the need for students to contribute to the cost of their education was concerns about pressures on the taxpayer. Lunt (2008) explained that the major expansion of student numbers that took place between 1987 and 1997, when the age cohort participation rate more than doubled, from around 15% to 33%, and thus the amount paid by the government to universities per student (the 'unit of resource') had been effectively halved. The continuous expansion, including the end of the 'binary divide', had created less certainty as to the nature and purpose of HE. Dearing was expected to provide solutions to the challenge of financing HE and to find a politically acceptable way of introducing a student contribution to tuition fees. It fundamentally changed the relationship between HE institutions and their students. Increasing participation was deemed necessary, and the positioning of students as paying users paved the way for further market-inspired policy changes.

However, the Dearing Report did highlight the considerable intrinsic value of HE outside market values despite the introduction of tuition fees. Continued public funding was justified on the grounds of the public goods associated with HE.

We do not accept a purely instrumental approach to higher education. Its distinctive character must lie in the independent pursuit of knowledge and understanding. But higher education has become central to the economic wellbeing of nations and individuals. (Dearing, 1997, p. 51)

The four main purposes of HE stated in the report were the following:

- *to inspire and enable individuals to develop their capabilities to the highest potential levels throughout life, so that they grow intellectually, are well-equipped for work, can contribute effectively to society and achieve personal fulfilment*

- *to increase knowledge and understanding for their own sake and to foster their application to the benefit of the economy and society*
- *to serve the needs of an adaptable, sustainable, knowledge-based economy at local, regional and national levels*
- *to play a major role in shaping a democratic, civilised, inclusive society* (Dearing, 1997, p. 72).

We can see here that three of these goals are non-economic and intrinsic. Another milestone of the Blair and Brown governments was the 2004 HE Act 2004, which introduced 'topup' or variable tuition fees up to £3,000 from 2006, which universities were permitted to introduce provided that they signed up to an 'Access Agreement' with the new Office for Fair Access (OFFA). The perceived private economic benefits started to come more to the fore. As Shattock (2013, p. 165) commented, "although Dearing had begun the process, the 2004 decision was a much more complete overturning of the Robbins framework where HE was regarded as sufficiently a public good to require a full financial subsidy for all students engaged in it". In 2009, *Higher Ambitions: The Future of Universities in a Knowledge Economy* (DBIS, 2009) further highlighted a need for universities to promote students' employability and answer employers' demands for skills further cementing the transactional relationship between students and institutions (Tholen, 2022).

Although New Labour's continued public funding was justified on paper on the grounds that there were extensive public goods associated with higher education, the instrumental interpretation of what a university should achieve was further solidified through the introduction of tuition fees and the performance-driven nature of HE management. The increasing relevance of HE as providing workforce skills and the perceived tightening between HE participation and perceived individual employability were also highlighted. Although New Labour proposed variable tuition fees and greater marketisation, the HE market was still based predominantly on differentiation rather than real competition (McCaig, 2018). No actual market occurred, and the increase in fees remained relatively low. But more radical change was about to come.

Tories: Cameron and May

That conservative governments would further dismantle the public character of HE is perhaps unsurprising. In response to the Browne Review, the 2011 White Paper *Higher Education: Students at the Heart of the*

System (DBIS, 2011) announced that the government would radically reduce government funding to HE institutions and install significantly higher tuition fees repaid via loans. It applied a cap of £9,000 per annum for full-time courses and £6,500 for part-time courses. In the document, the demand for HE is explicitly linked to market demand, which was still deemed larger than the number of places available (Tholen, 2022). In 2014, the government removed all controls on domestic student numbers (in England).

The 2016 White Paper titled *Success as a Knowledge Economy* marks another important milestone in HE reform. It further aimed to improve the accessibility and quality of HE courses through the Teaching Excellence Framework (TEF), which assesses universities' quality of student experience, teaching standards, and labour market outcomes for graduates. Teaching quality, learning environment, student outcomes, and learning gain were the key aspects of measuring quality in which performance management mechanisms would function (DBIS, 2016). As such, it reduced the objective of HE as a function of consumer judgement. In particular, the inclusion of labour market outcomes as a criterion of quality teaching has been criticised (Tholen, 2018). This narrowing down of previous intrinsic ideals of the university is strengthened by the creation of the Office for Students (OfS) as a result of the Higher Education and Research Act 2017. It regulates the student market, oversees whether competition and choice are expressed in the system, and assesses quality and standards.

The 2019 Augar Review continued the concern about value for money and the commodification of HE. It also continued to place university education against labour market skill demands. It argued that university funding should move away from those seen as 'low value' and be targeted towards high-cost subjects and high-demand priority areas (Adams, 2022).

The gradual increase in undergraduate tuition fees in English HE was sold politically as natural and inevitable given the state of public finance, particularly after the 2008 financial crisis. A related long-serving populist argument is that a funding system that privileged university students was unfair to those who did not attend university, whose taxes were paying for those who do. Browne's argument for higher fees was that the direct benefits are mainly with the graduate, and HE is neither compulsory nor universal, so it is an individual's choice to participate (Carasso & Locke, 2015, p. 32). Further arguments around the importance of student choice were also compelling. HE institutions became competitors in a quasi-market, competing for students on quality and value for money. The competition on price never materialised, as all HE institutions started to charge the maximum tuition fee for home undergraduate students (around £9,000, frozen at £9,250 per year since 2017). As McCaig (2018, p. 95) highlighted, the financial risk shifted from the state to institutions and students. Shattock (2012, p. 168) argued that the history of tuition fees also tells us a great deal about the involvement of the state in British universities, which have historically claimed considerable legal institutional independence. Between 1945 and 2004, state-controlled and manipulated fees were used for policy purposes. Yet, despite the financial autonomy from the state that came with the increase in fees, it did not increase the autonomy of universities elsewhere.

Whether tuition increases in fees were ideological or merely pragmatic money-saving measures, they have strengthened the economic-instrumental idea of a university. More economic-instrumental aims slowly overtook the non-instrumental aims of HE outlined earlier. They were as follows:

- Increase societal economic gains (growth/productivity)
- Raise personal, tangible gains, such as improved labour market outcome (wage and employment) and employability
- Creation of knowledge for economic purposes

The dominance of the economic-instrumental view of HE did not happen overnight but has been slowly fading. Under the influence of human capital theory, policymakers in the last few decades showed much more interest in the economic benefits of HE to support policy, and this received far more attention than the non-economic ones (Mandler, 2020). Yet we can say that in the British context, it accelerated in the 1960s, and by the 2000s, the instrumental view of what HE should be about had largely overtaken the intrinsic one. The decline of the intrinsic view of HE was perhaps compromised by the emergence of new institutions with possibly a broader set of aims, perhaps also shifting the idea of the university.

Conclusion: The Ideal of a University

This chapter has demonstrated a change in how universities are perceived. It is convenient to deduce that universities have always shared an essential element, but there seems to be a co-existence between a non-instrument idealist understanding and a more utilitarian approach to understanding the idea of the university. As Collini (2017, p. 17) conceded, "[W]e should certainly begin by recognizing that universities have always in part served practical ends and have always helped to prepare their graduates for employment later in life". He also pointed out that there is a fair bit of romanticism, idealism, and nostalgia wrapped in the account of the non-economic intrinsic aims. Palleyfrey and Tapper (2014) argued that vocationalism has always been a crucial part of UK universities. The generous public funding of HE only covers a few decades and is more an exception than the rule. State-funded research likewise only took off early in the twentieth century. Yet this is not to say that there has not been a real change in how HE and its universities have been understood over time. As John and Fanghanel (2016, p. 3) observed, the focus of successive governments on the economic contribution of universities has somewhat left aside any consideration of the university's educational and social functions.

Over time, the non-instrumental and non-economic aims that dominate university education have shifted within the policy landscape. Despite Robbins's flirtations with neoliberal ideas in other areas, the report still portrayed HE mainly as a public good. As the demand for HE grew, Robbins's response to it marked the first real sign of what was to come, but it was not until Margaret Thatcher's introduction of quasi-markets that intrinsic understandings of HE seemed to wither. Although it was an accepted economic resource, HE remained largely academic and non-vocational until the 1970s, when greater political interest in the economic pay-off of university education was highlighted (King, 2003, p. 15). From 1979 onwards, successive governments emphasised that HE should foremost be seen as a personal investment and an economic imperative in a globalised world.

The economic-instrumental aims of HE are supported by what has been dubbed the "economic ideology of higher education" (Salter & Tapper, 1994), which stresses that the principal role of HE is to serve the economy and, in particular, to contribute to national competitiveness. This has been made possible by governments exerting more control over public expenditure on HE. Marketisation made much more sense once universities were seen in an economic frame. Policy changes over time have made universities act within a market-like system. Universities are encouraged to compete for students but also research income from government and non-government sources. Their economic survival rested on their commercial and market instincts, to the extent that "[T]he only remnants of public service was a concern, largely rhetorical, to try to achieve some measure of equity in student participation" (Williams, 2016a, p. 135). Why this has changed is largely related to how universities have been managed by the state. As Williams (2016b, p. 625) observed,

> As relatively autonomous institutions, universities had been mainly free from state interference and able to set their own broadly liberal academic priorities, admission criteria and overall sense of purpose. Increased state funding, motivated by a desire to promote the public good, opened up universities to greater direction from national government.

The underlying rationale behind the unification of the HE system in England in 1992 was, in part, to encourage greater competition in the HE sector, where students did not immediately come to be seen as consumers in an ordinary sense. However, HE has ultimately become akin to an investment good, with labour market outcome data provided to help make the right investment (Britton et al., 2020; Tholen, 2022). The Office for Students now protects students' consumer interests and legally, the relationship between HE institutions and students became contractualised after the Higher Education Act (2004). Both Labour and Conservative governments have forced HE institutions to operate under government-influenced market conditions (Tapper & Palleyfrey, 2014).

It is important to observe that, historically, the essence of HE was far from set in stone. President of the University of California Clark Kerr, in 1963, for example, famously called the modern university a 'multiversity' to capture these different functions and the different communities of interest they expressed (Kerr, 1963). Robbins suggested that "there is no single aim which, if pursued to the exclusion of all others, would not leave out essential elements. Eclecticism in this sphere is not something to be despised; it is imposed by the circumstances of the case. To do justice to the complexity of things, it is necessary to acknowledge a plurality of aims" (Robbins, 1963, para 23). However, over time, the wider aims of HE moved out of sight. Nonetheless, the debate on what the 'idea' of a university ought to be has not gone away with the dominance of the instrumental economic view. The change did not go unnoticed, and many have strong moral reservations regarding the economic instrument aims that dominate the modern university. According to Readings (1996, p. 19), the US university has lost its historical 'raison d'être'. He claimed that "[T]he university [...] no longer participates in the historical project for humanity that was the legacy of the Enlightenment". Ashwin (2020, p. 9) stated that economic arguments dominate our thinking about the purpose and nature of higher education, and we need to highlight alternative purposes of HE. He contended that HE should not be about graduate salaries but about the contribution that graduates make to the cohesiveness of their societies (p. 126).

Over time, resistance like this has grown, with critical voices often choosing to frame it as a fight against neoliberalism. Neoliberalism is seen to have affected many institutions in society, and HE is another victim of its enduring impact on the social world. The next chapter examines how we can understand such a cavernous concept. To do so, we need to look at the concept more closely and understand the heterogeneity of its use.

Note

1. HE expansion had already set in, as pointed out by Willetts (2017).

References

Adams, R. (2022). England and Wales university fees 'bad value for money' – survey. *The Guardian*, August 31. https://www.theguardian.com/education/2022/aug/31/england-and-wales-university-feesbad-value-for-money-survey

Anderson, R. (2006). *British Universities Past and Present*. Bloomsbury.

Anderson, R. (2010). *The 'Idea of a University' Today. History and Policy. Policy Papers.* Retrieved April 22, 2024, from https://www.historyandpolicy.org/policy-papers/papers/the-idea-of-a-university-today

Ashwin, P. (2020). *Transforming University Education: A Manifesto*. Bloomsbury.

Bradley, S., Draca, M., & Green, C. (2004). School performance in Australia: Is there a role for quasimarkets? *Australian Economic Review*, 37(3), 271–286.

Britton, J., Dearden, L., van der Erve, L. L., & Waltmann, B. (2020). *The Impact of Undergraduate Degrees on Lifetime Earnings*. IFS.

Brown, P., & Lauder, H. (2001). *Capitalism and Social Progress: The Future of Society in a Global Economy*. Palgrave.

Carasso, H., & Locke, W. (2015). Paying the price of expansion: Why more for undergraduates in England means less for everyone. In P. John & J. Fanghanel (Eds.), *Dimensions of Marketisation in Higher Education* (pp. 26–37). Routledge.

Carpentier, V. (2015). The historical expansion of higher education in Europe: Spaces, shapes and rationales. In J. L. Rury & E. H. Tamura (Eds.), *The Oxford Handbook of The History of Education* (pp. 259–274). Oxford University Press.

Carpentier, V. (2018). Expansion and differentiation in higher education: The historical trajectories of the UK, the USA and France. In *CGHE Working Paper 33*. Centre for Global Higher Education.
Carpentier, V. (2019). Higher education in modern Europe. In J. L. Rury & E. H. Tamura (Eds.), *The Oxford Handbook of The History of Education* (pp. 259–274). Oxford University Press.
Clark, W. (2006). *Academic Charisma and the Origins of the Research University*. University of Chicago Press.
Clarke, J., Newman, J., & Westmarland, L. (2007). The antagonisms of choice: New Labour and the reform of public services. *Social Policy & Society, 7*(2), 245–253.
Coates, K. (2016). Playing to the numbers. *Prometheus, 34*(1), 73–77.
Collini, S. (2012). *What Are Universities For?* Penguin.
Collini, S. (2013). Sold out. *London Review of Books, 35*(20), 3–12.
Collini, S. (2017). *Speaking of Universities*. Verso Books.
Dearing, R. (1997). *Higher Education in the Learning Society*. HMSO.
Department for Business, Innovation and Skills (DBIS). (2009). *Higher Ambitions: The Future of Universities in a Knowledge Economy*. London.
Department for Business, Innovation and Skills (DBIS). (2011). *Students at the Heart of the System*. London.
Department for Business Innovation and Skills (DBIS). (2016). *Success as a Knowledge Economy: Teaching Excellence, Social Mobility and Student Choice*. HM Government.
DES. (1991). *Education and Training for the Twenty-First Century* (Vol. 2 vols). HMSO.
Driver, S., & Martell, L. (2006). *New Labour* (2nd ed.). Polity Press.
Edwards, K. (*2004*). The university in Europe and the US. In R. King (Ed.), *The University in the Global Age* (pp. 27–44). Palgrave Macmillan.
Evans, G. R. (2018). University': The history of the search for a definition in England. In M. Feingold (Ed.), *History of Universities: Volume XXXI* (pp. 187–212). Oxford University Press.
Ferlie, E., Musselin, C., & Andresani, G. (2009). The governance of higher education systems: A public management prespective. In C. Paradeise, E. Reale, I. Bleiklie, & E. Ferlie (Eds.), *University Governance: Western European Comparative Perspective* (pp. 1–19). Springer.
Fitz, J., & Hafid, T. (2007). Perspectives on the privatization of public schooling in England and Wales. *Educational Policy, 21*(1), 273–296.
Greener, I. (2008). Choice and voice – a review. *Social Policy and Society, 7*(2), 255–265.
Habermas, J. (1987a). *The University in a Democracy: Democratization of the University. Toward a Rational Society* (pp. 1–12). Polity Press.

Habermas, J. (1987b). The idea of the university – learning processess. *New German Critique, 41*, 3–22.
Holmwood, J. (2014). From social rights to the market: Neoliberalism and the knowledge economy. *International Journal of Lifelong Education, 33*(1), 62–76.
Jaspers, K. (1961). *The Idea of a University*. Peter Owen.
John, P., Fanghanel, J., & J. (2016). 'Fearful symmetry?' Higher education and the logic of the market. In P. John & J. Fanghanel (Eds.), *Dimensions of Marketisation in Higher Education* (pp. 1–12). Routledge.
Kelly, P., Fair, N., & Evans, C. (2017). The engaged student ideal in UK higher education policy. *High Education Policy, 30*, 105–122.
Kerr, C. (1963). *The Uses of the University*. Harvard University Press.
King, R. (2003). *The University in the Global Age*. Palgrave Macmillan.
Lambert, H. (2019). The great university con: How the British degree lost its value. *The New Statesman*, August 13. Retrieved April 22, 2024, from https://www.newstatesman.com/politics/2019/08/the-great-university-con-how-the-british-degree-lost-its-value
Le Grand, J. (2007). *The Other Invisible Hand: Delivering Public Services through Choice and Competition*. Princeton University Press.
Lovlie, L., & Standish, P. (2003). Introduction: Bildung and the idea of a liberal education. In L. Lovlie, K. P. Mortensenand, & S. E. Nordenbo (Eds.), *Educating Humanity: Bildung in Postmodernity* (pp. 1–24). Blackwell.
Lowe, R. (Ed.). (2008). *The History of Higher Education*. Routledge.
Lunt, I. (2008). Beyond tuition fees? The legacy of Blair's government to higher education. *Oxford Review of Education, 34*(6), 741–752.
Mandler, P. (2020). *The Crisis of the Meritocracy. Britain's Transition to Mass Education Since the Second World War*. Oxford University Press.
Mayhew, K., Deer, C., & Dua, M. (2004). The move to mass higher education in the UK: Many questions and some answers. *Oxford Review of Education, 30*(1), 65–82.
McCaig, C. (2018). *The Marketisation of English Higher Education: A Policy Analysis of a Risk-Based System*. Emerald.
Newman, J. H. (1996). *The Idea of a University*. Mcmackin Garland, M. et al. (eds.): Yale University Press.
Nussbaum, M. C. (1997). *Cultivating Humanity: A Classical Defense of Reform in Liberal Education*. Harvard University Press.
O'Day, R. (2009). Universities and professions in the early modern period. In P. Cunningham, S. Oosthuizen, & R. Taylor (Eds.), *Beyond the Lecture Hall Universities and Community Engagement from the Middle Ages to the Present Day* (pp. 79–102). University of Cambridge Faculty of Education and Institute of Continuing Education.

Palfreyman, D., & Tapper, T. (2014). *Reshaping the University: The Rise of the Regulated Market in Higher Education*. Oxford University Press.
Pedersen O. (1998). *The First Universities: Studium Generale and the Origins of University Education in Europe* (North R, Trans.). Cambridge: Cambridge University Press.
Perkin, H. (2007). History of universities. In J. J. F. Forest & P. G. Altbach (Eds.), *Handbook of Higher Education* (pp. 159–206). Springer.
Peters, A. M. & R. Barnett (eds.) (2018). *The Idea of the University: A Reader (Vol. I)*. Peter Lang.
Readings, B. (1996). *The University in Ruins*. Harvard University Press.
de Ridder-Symoens, H. (1992). *A History of the University in Europe. Vol. I. Universities in the Middle Ages*. Cambridge University Press.
Robbins, L. (1963). *Higher Education: Report of the Committee Appointed by the Prime Minister under the Chairmanship of Lord Robbins, Cmnd. 2154*. HMSO.
Rothblatt, S. (1997). *The Modern University and its Discontents: The Fate of Newman's Legacies in Britain and America*. Cambridge University Press.
Rustin, M. (2016). The neoliberal university and its alternatives. *Soundings*, 63(63), 147–176.
Salter, B., & Tapper, T. (1994). *The State and Higher Education*. The Woburn Press.
Sanderson, M. (1972). *The Universities and British Industry 1850–1970*. Routledge & Kegan Paul.
Scott, P. (2021). *Retreat or Resolution? Tackling the Crisis of Mass Higher Education*. University of Bristol Press.
Shattock, M. (2008). The change from private to public governance of British higher education: Its consequences for higher education policy making 1980–2006. *Higher Education Quarterly*, 62(3), 181–203.
Shattock, M. (2012). *Making Policy in British Higher Education: 1945–2011*. Routledge.
Shattock, M. (2013). University governance, leadership and management in a decade of diversification and uncertainty. *Higher Education Quarterly*, 67(3), 217–233.
Sørensen, A. (2015). From critique of ideology to politics: Habermas on Bildung. *Ethics and Education*, 10(2), 252–270.
Tholen, G. (2014). *The Changing Nature of the Graduate Labour Market: Media, Policy and Political Discourses in the UK*. Palgrave Macmillan.
Tholen, G. (2018). University isn't the be all and end all when it comes to employment outcomes. *The Conversation*, October 4. Retrieved April 24, 2024, from https://theconversation.com/university-isnt-the-be-all-and-end-all-when-it-comes-to-employment-outcomes-103180
Tholen, G. (2022). *Modern Work and the Marketisation of Higher Education*. Policy Press Bristol.

Tomlinson, S. (2001). Education policy, 1997–2000: The effects on top, bottom and middle England, International. *Studies in Sociology of Education, 11*(3), 261–278.

Whitty, G. (2009). The legacy of neo-liberal school reform in England. *Comparative Education, 39*, 3–28.

Willetts, D. (2017). *A University Education*. Oxford University Press.

Williams, G. (2013). A bridge too far: An economic critique of marketization of higher education. In C. Callender & P. Scott (Eds.), *Browne and Beyond: Modernizing English Higher Education* (pp. 57–72). Institute of Education Press.

Williams, G. (2016a). Higher education: Public good or private commodity? *London Review of Education, 14*(1), 131–142.

Williams, J. (2016b). A critical exploration of changing definitions of public good in relation to higher education. *Studies in Higher Education, 41*(4), 619–630.

CHAPTER 3

How Can We Understand Neoliberalism?

Abstract This chapter examines the concept of neoliberalism. It consists of two parts. The first part offers an intellectual history of key neoliberal thinkers and ideas. It covers the Austrian and Chicago Schools as well as proponents of public choice theory. The second part distinguishes three ways neoliberalism has been understood. These three are neoliberalism as (a) policy, (b) ideology, and (c) governmentality.

Keywords Neoliberalism • Policy • Ideology • Governmentality

To assess the extent to which neoliberalism has driven the marketisation of HE, clarity is needed about what we mean by neoliberalism. To do so, this chapter offers a historical grounding and a conceptual analysis of how the concept is used, presenting three main applications that will serve as an analytical framework for the next chapters. These three uses are neoliberalism as (a) policy, (b) ideology, and (c) governmentality.

© The Author(s), under exclusive license to Springer Nature Switzerland AG 2024
G. Tholen, *The Role of Neoliberalism in the Marketisation of Higher Education*, Palgrave Studies on Global Policy and Critical Futures in Education, https://doi.org/10.1007/978-3-031-66281-2_3

Short History of Neoliberal Thought

To understand the concept of neoliberalism, a historical overview of its intellectual roots can help contextualise its influence on education. In particular, its sudden rise in the 1980s may suggest that a new economic philosophy entered the marketplace of ideas. But before that, a long period of early modest popularity served as an important period in its existence as a variety of streams appeared that were directly in conversation with each other. What follows is only a brief and descriptive overview. Neoliberalism is not static or even coherent, as Mirowski (2013) explained. Yet there are some principles, assumptions, and concepts that played a central role in intellectual history. More detailed and analytical genealogies are found in, for instance, Mirowski and Plehwe (2009), Burgin (2012), Kiely (2018), and Stedman Jones (2012).

Neoliberalism as an intellectual movement and political theoretical project originated in the interwar period, in the 1920s and 1930s, as economists, philosophers, and political scientists were brought together by their agreement on the failure of classical liberalism and an existential anxiety of liberalism. The perceived crisis of liberalism was deeply grounded within this period when the atrocities of war and the rise of totalitarian anti-liberal political forces were deeply felt as anti-liberal. Also, state planning sustained in both world wars and the Great Depression was at the basis of the perception that liberalism was in crisis. In particular, the growing welfare states and economic involvement of the state in the economy were seen as politically accepted (Biebrichter, 2018). The economic contractions and failures of the Great Depression caused the popularity of interventionist and collectivist political ideas and a loss of confidence in free markets and laissez-faire economics. Classical liberalism had also lost its legitimacy in society, and returning to it was neither possible nor desirable. Neoliberalism as an intellectual movement came very much as a response to reformulate liberalism, as a renewal of the case for economic liberalism, and a countermovement against Keynesiasm. Founding thinkers such as Ludwig von Mises and Friedrich Hayek set themselves the task of reimagining economic liberalism in new ways to accommodate the new circumstances and effectively combat political collectivist movements, including Stalinist state socialism, German and Italian fascism, the New Deal in the United States, and, to varying degrees, Keynesian liberalism.

These issues were debated by scholars at the Walter Lippmann Colloquium in 1938, which French philosopher Louis Rougier organised in Paris in honour of the American journalist Lipmann, a vocal critic of the New Deal. Years later, in 1947, a small group of intellectuals met at the Hotel du Parc in Mont Pèlerin, Switzerland. This was the start of a global intellectual movement that over time penetrated political spheres all over the world through various means (including powerful think tanks) (Mirowski & Plehwe, 2009). The key organiser of that meeting, Friedrich Hayek, together with economist Milton Friedman, were soon to become prominent thinkers of what was to be called neoliberalism. This first generation of neoliberal thinkers convened in Paris for the Walter Lippmann Colloquium. They brought back some elements of the previous liberal agenda while abandoning others (Biebricher, 2018). One of the defining features was its emphasis on competition, which is a political and economic good through which political and economic freedom can be achieved (Mises, 2007; Hayek, 2002).

Earlier intellectual foundations can be found in the writings of Ludwig von Mises and those adhering to ordoliberalism, which emerged in Freiburg in the 1930s. Ordoliberals such as Eucken and Ropke were often linked with neoliberalism and had already written about a possible liberal order beyond laissez-faire. It emphasised the importance of free-market competition as a guarantor of political rights, theorising how the state could actively establish a competitive order. Far from the laissez-faire ideology of the past, ordoliberals argued not only against the concentration of state power associated with totalitarian regimes but also the concentration of private economic power (in particular, the rise of cartels), which resulted from laissez-faire capitalism. A strong state could facilitate and promote market competition, entrepreneurship, private property, and the price mechanism, which were deemed central features of a free society.

What follows from these original movements is the wide variety of contributions that have formed the intellectual tradition of neoliberalism. I will touch upon some main strands and authors within the neoliberal movement to outline some key ideas and how they are connected to other eachother. It is important to note again that these by no means form a complete history of ideas within the neoliberal tradition. It is often argued that neoliberal thought came to solidify around three dominant intellectual influences: Austrian economics, the Chicago School, and public choice theory (see Birch, (2015) for a discussion of other strands not covered here). We will start with the Austrian School and its prime exponent, Hayek.

Hayek and the Austrian School of Economics

The Austrian School of neoliberal thought emerged around Carl Menger, Friedrich Wieser, and Eugene Böhm-Bawerk in the late nineteenth century, and later Ludwig von Mises and Friedrich von Hayek. Their work on the subjective theory of value and the political defence of laissez-faire economic policy became a key pillar in neoliberalism. I will focus on the work of Hayek, who was a most influential proponent of the Austrian School and was frequently seen as the founding father of neoliberalism. Hayek's philosophy is wide-ranging, and some have successfully digested it (e.g. Caldwell, 2004; Feser, 2006). Hayek has changed position over his lifetime, but some key themes run through his work.

The first is the idea of the central position of consumer choice in the expression of being human. Hayek (1948, p. 110) stated that "competition can be made more effective and more beneficent by certain government activities than it would be without them". Hayek here drew on the Austrian School's subjective theory of value, which states that the value of a good is not determined by any inherent property of the good or labour value but by the individual importance towards that good. There can be no scientific account of human need but only of consumer preference. Any choice based on moral principles is not qualitatively different from choices based on economic principles, such as the pursuit of wealth or efficiency. However, Hayek departed from the idea that individuals should be seen as *Homo oeconomicus*, in other words, rational and acting through the calculus of maximisation to make calculations based on the available data. Hayek explained how choice, rather than maximalisation, defines an economic actor. Choice within the market is dynamic and creative; ultimately, it is how the subject can learn and act rationally and govern themselves, for individuals within the market find themselves ignorant. However, the market mechanism provides knowledge directly utilisable in the market, creating profitable opportunities. As seen in markets, local knowledge is always more valid and effective than other forms of knowledge in economic planning.

One of the fundamental strengths of the market is that it offers individuals the freedom to get what each believes is of value. Its price mechanism mediates between all rival perspectives and values (Hayek, 1944, pp. 51–52). The market is a knowledge-processing machine that is constantly at work and evolving. It reveals truth that no individual or scientific endeavour could ever achieve. This is part of a broader scepticism regarding the ability of human reason to understand the complexity of social phenomena. For Hayek, the market does not just facilitate trade in goods and services; it reveals truth and goes beyond the limits of human reason. Its spontaneous order is made up of countless individual actions, too complex for market actors to understand. As a kind of supercomputer, the market transmits crucial information about the actions of many individuals. The market coordinates individual needs and resources, generating new knowledge which no individual could capture, and is a fundamentally neutral price mechanism that mediates between all rival perspectives and values. It is thus above the actions of any one individual. Market outcomes should not be justified by fairness or merit but as a result of an economic order that is the most productive and efficient in maximising average individual income and opportunities (Hayek, 1976).

Hayek's comprehension of the market was part of a wider understanding of phenomena. Hayek (1973, pp. 35–54) distinguished 'taxis'—a deliberately constructed order, such as a state—and 'cosmos'—a spontaneous order that is the product not of design but of evolution, such as a market. Self-organising and self-replicating structures emerge without design, constantly changing the process of tending towards orderliness. The market is an organic and spontaneous order; markets are therefore natural phenomena to be observed throughout the natural world (Hayek, 1967, 1973, 1976). It is the market where knowledge resides, and the individual can be ignorant and still be a successful market actor. Hayek opined, "The most significant fact about this system is the economy of knowledge with which it operates, or how little the individual participants need to know in order to be able to take the right action" (Hayek, 1945, p. 527).

Perhaps unsurprisingly, Hayek believed that the market should be allowed to function freely, with free individuals making their own decisions about how to allocate their resources, ensuring that the knowledge and expertise required for efficient decision-making would be brought together in an effective manner. He argued that attempts by the state to intervene in the economy would inevitably limit individual freedom, as the state would be making decisions about the use of resources that should be left to individuals. Because of its distinct advantages over state regulation or planning, the market has no alternative. State intervention is a constructed order and *necessarily* reduces both market efficiency as well as individual freedom.

Hayek's ideas of politics and the state are also key to his philosophy. The rule of law and the maintenance of market order are two of the fundamental roles of the state, in Hayek's view. *The Road to Serfdom* was a warning that collectivist systems oppose competition (Hayek, 1944, p. 42). Their economic planning ignores how the market processes knowledge and interferes with the self-regulating mechanism of the market. Efficient economic planning is impossible, as it suppresses market prices. In a free-market economy, they act as information signal about the dispersed preferences of many buyers and sellers. The state can never account for the individual desires and rationalisations that often remain inaccessible and tacit and compete with the power of ignorance that free markets provide. Its intention to represent people is doomed to fail. There are clear similarities between the market and society for Hayek. Both are highly complex 'spontaneous orders' and an aggregation of individuals, each of whom acts according to their own individual purposes. There is no overall purpose that can be determined. Similarly, society's flexibility and vitality should not be restricted; attempts to 'control' it are again misguided.

State planning of any sort is incompatible with how markets function. It is inefficient, as the state does not hold the locally generated knowledge market and threatens individual freedom (Hayek, 1944). Hayek also argued sharply against welfare state arguments (Hayek, 1944) and the perceived need to extend the state's role within society and economy to ensure distributive justice and greater equality. These policies disturb the market, as they prevent access to equal opportunity in the market and the transmission of accurate market signal information. According to Hayek, they also cause state dependency and represent a real threat to freedom. Citizens serve the government rather than themselves. Hayek did not think that an unequal distribution or lack of economic resources limits the achievement of freedom. Distributive justice fundamentally means treating individuals differently, which does not make sense, is unjust within a free market, and will damage individual freedom. The state needs to treat each individual the same instead of treating those that "differ greatly in strength, intelligence, skill, knowledge and perseverance" differently (Hayek, 1976, p. 82). According to Hayek, economic freedom has nothing to do with achieving equality in people's skills, capacities, incomes, and wealth. The value of freedom is the same for all members of society.

However, the state has a clear role in maintaining the legal system. According to Hayek, providing a legal framework is essential for the market to work effectively. Hayek was sceptical of state action that goes beyond the *minimal* functions of national defence, the protection of basic rights to life and property, and the enforcement of contracts, as they often become threats to liberty. Yet the role of the state for Hayek is removed from the minimal watchman state; even economic intervention is allowed if it aids the competition under the rule of law. As the market is not functioning perfectly, the state must correct imperfections. And so the 'invisible hand' works when individual action is constrained by the powers of law or custom, as long as it serves the functioning of the market. He stated, "It is the character rather than the volume of government activity that is important. A functioning market economy presupposes certain activities on the part of the state; there are some other such activities by which its functioning will be assisted; and it can tolerate many more, provided that they are of the kind which are compatible with a functioning market" (Hayek, 2006, p. 194). Other state policies, including taxation, the provision of collective goods, the correction of externalities, and the financing of education, can be justified if they do not restrict price competition. Even public services in education, health, or public infrastructures can be acceptable if the state has no monopoly and competes with private providers (Hayek, 2006). Hayek argued for an active state guided by sound economic analysis and the rule of law (Hayek, 1944).

However, the state should be deliberately neutral and ignorant and not only refrain from obstructing it but reinvent itself to guarantee the market can remain agnostic and impartial. To pursue moral goals on behalf of society via the state, on the other hand, is to claim knowledge of the desires and values of others. Hence, only scientific-moral agnosticism is truly liberal. It is important to note that Hayek's position has changed over his lifetime, particularly from the 1960s onwards, and some of his positions oscillate between libertarianism and conservatism.

Chicago School and Friedman

From the 1950s, a distinctive form of neoliberal thought developed at the University of Chicago, led by intellectuals including Milton Friedman, George Stigler, Aaron Director, Frank Knight, and later, Gary Becker and Ronald Coase (Van Horn et al., 2013; Nik-Khah & van Horn, 2016). The 'Chicago School', as it came to be known, was intellectually more grounded in neoclassical economics than the Austrian School. Market actors were positioned as rational, self-interested, utility-maximising agents with stable preferences, interacting through equilibrating markets.

Like the Austrian School, it was strongly anti-Keynesian and similarly considered the market a highly efficient mechanism for allocating resources. The interaction of buyers and sellers in a market leads to mutually beneficial outcomes, all made possible by the price mechanism, which signals market actors about the relative scarcity of goods and services. The market is capable of self-regulation, maximising efficient outcomes without government intervention. One of the key principles of the Chicago School's understanding of the market is defined by rational self-interest. Market actors naturally act on self-interest, pursuing their own goals and preferences. This leads to the efficient allocation of resources, benefitting all.

Friedman

As an economist, Milton Friedman was influential, particularly in monetary policy and his ideas on the role of government in the economy, and argued for self-regulation of markets and deregulation to promote innovation and market competition. In *Capitalism and Freedom*, Friedman (1962) considered a free-market economy as essential to safeguard individual freedom from government intervention. The state's role should be limited to protecting property rights and enforcing contracts. Friedman also advocated for deregulation, arguing that unnecessary government regulations could stifle innovation and competition and ultimately threaten freedom. Effectively, Friedman always preferred market solutions over governmental solutions, pointing out the potential efficiency of the market, even if it leads to monopolies or non-market agreements.

There are some critical differences between Hayek and Friedman. We can see significant differences in the role of knowledge within the economy, as well as the role of the state. Hayek questioned the possibility of any centralised authoritative economic knowledge and claimed that no amount of intellect can overcome the inherent limits to knowledge in human social and economic systems. For Friedman and the Chicago School, bureaucratic and calculative power could be a basis for better and more efficient decision making. For instance, powerful and intelligent firms are treated as positive. Hayek put greater emphasis on the ignorance and the knowledge located in the market. Chicago economists envisaged action governed by neoclassical calculation, potentially quite sophisticated calculation, not least by the state. There are also some differences in the role of the state. Hayek is more tolerant of interventions to support the free market, consistent with the principles of the rule of law and neutral, abstract in nature. Hayek gives the state more room to defend competitive freedoms, and his work shows much more flexibility, but always in support of the coordination mechanisms of the market. For Friedman, the main role of the government is national protection and the upholding of law and order. After this, some government activity is allowed under strict scrutiny if it increases efficiency. In *Capitalism and Freedom*, Friedman (1962) is clear that forces of the free market, when left to their own devices, would spontaneously produce the best possible outcomes.

For Friedman, state intervention is illegitimate, apart from where they create and enforce a set of rules for market conduct, overcome 'neighbourhood effects' where one actor's economic activity imposes a cost on another actor (e.g. pollution) or where they need to act on 'paternalistic grounds' on behalf of those individuals who are either unable to recognise or to act on their own preferences (Friedman, 1962, pp. 27–34). In most other cases, governments would likely damage the freedom of market actors' transactions (Schmidt, 2018). There is also a refusal to accept that market failure is even possible.

The Chicago School demonstrated a firm belief in the capacity of economics to explain all forms of human behaviour. It included economic strands such as search theory (Stigler), human capital theory (Becker), and transaction cost analysis (Coase). All three theories are concerned with understanding market behaviour and, in particular, analysing the decision-making processes of economic agents. The Chicago School's economic approach, particularly Friedman's normative preference for free markets and limited government, was applied to other areas of the economy and, increasingly, to society and social phenomena. Or, as Foucault interpreted it, a "generalisation of the economic form of the market ... throughout the social body" (Foucault, 2008, p. 243). This was most evident in the works of Becker, who argued that "the economic approach is a comprehensive one that is applicable to all human behavior" (Becker, 1990, p. 8), who then applied it to non-economic phenomena, such as marriage, crime, and addiction.

Public Choice

The third intellectual strand covered here is strongly associated with the Chicago School. The Virginia School of Political Economy (or Virginia School) developed 'public choice theory', which underpins a new set of neoliberal ideas. Together with Gordon Tullock James Buchanan can be seen as the key intellectual in this strand. The public choice theory view of the market departs from earlier neoliberal conceptualisations. For Hayek, markets are a spontaneous societal order for which there are no alternatives to compute practical fragmented knowledge, especially not by forces that inflict centralised planning. Unregulated markets express freedom and spark creativity and progress. Buchanan (1975) was far less optimistic that the market process alone would necessarily promote harmony and progress. Conscious action through the state to achieve freedom and prosperity is needed. In Buchanan's view, markets are a useful technology for the state. He distinguishes between the 'protective state' and the 'productive state'. The former is concerned with the basic constitutional framework of rights enforced by law and with national defence; it protects the core rights of citizens via internal security, contract enforcement, and defence against external threats. The protective state represents constitutional safeguards to radically change the status quo in rights and protection. The productive state arises from citizens agreeing to pool their resources to collectively produce public goods that cannot be produced individually or through regular market activity. In *The Limits of Liberty*, Buchanan (1975) supported some redistribution; his proposed social contract of a 'productive' state includes tax-financed goods and some social insurance. In these cases, they represent a collective agreement in which individuals exchange their tax payments for collectively produced outputs (e.g. infrastructure or parks).

The productive state is subject to choice and has 'evolved' over time into an illiberal and redistributive state. It intervenes in the private economy by promoting the same ends pursued in the private sector, leaving little meaningful distinction between public and private interests. The government has taken over many roles previously left to the markets. Governments are shaped by a coalition of voters who seek advantage through state action (including legislation). Modern politics consists predominantly of rent-seeking activities, transferring resources from one group to another through collective action. Over time, the welfare state and ever-growing government power have benefitted certain interest groups over others in a rent-seeking society, in which many look for investment in rent-seeking and rent protection. The concept of "rent-seeking" is also used by Tullock (1967) to theorise how businesses try to gain financial advantage through securing favourable legislative changes rather than engaging in competition with products or services.

According to public choice theory, the state is fundamentally dangerous and prone to misuse its powers. In practice, it more often than not exists to serve the interests of those who hold power. Government officials will attempt to expand government departments and programmes and increase government spending, leading to large deficits and inflation and expansion of government budgets and "empire building" (Buchanan et al., 1978). Politicians (and public sector workers generally) are not driven by public services. Instead, like everyone else, they are rational, calculating utility maximisers who act on self-interest. In other words, people act in the same way, whether in markets or politics. The school's 'economics of politics' contends that economic analysis should be applied to the political sphere. The public sphere is effectively de-politicisation, or 'de-democratisation'. Public choice theory argues that mechanisms such as constitutional constraints, transparency and accountability measures, and electoral competition can help to mitigate the risks of state capture and rent-seeking. The institutional regulation of the public sector and public governance should be based on the principles of the market, aligning the interests of political actors with the broader public interest. Promoting greater competition, transparency, and accountability may limit special interests. As we have seen with the Austrian and Chicago Schools, markets are better able to represent people's preferences than the state government. Public choice theory pleads for rolling back the state in favour of the private sector.

Neoliberalism in Practice: Institution Building and Political Influence

Moving away from these intellectual movements, we can see neoliberal ideas become solidified in the world beyond the so-called thought collective. They most clearly penetrated political circles, shaping national states and other governmental organisations above and below the nation-state and institutions (Mirowski & Plehwe, 2009; Stedman Jones, 2012). Neoliberal ideas migrated from the margins to the centre of political life as they came to shape global trade and development discourse, as well as the politics of powerful Western democracies (Chang, 2002). However, it took a while before neoliberal influence was felt within politics. It was not until the 1970s that the golden era of interventionism ended. The intellectual challenge against the idea that economies need active state involvement and states are responsible for their populations' welfare was, as we have seen, already there. It took considerable time to become influential because of the widespread acceptance and legitimacy of welfare economics, Keynesianism, and social-democratic politics. Interventionism and redistributive policies were promoted by a wide range of political parties, as well as strong labour movements.

There are many reasons why the trust in interventionism declined. There have been economic changes. The Bretton Woods system of fixed exchange rates, which supported the international financial system within which Keynesian macroeconomics operated, ended. A rapid growth of global financial flows led to the breakdown of domestic and international financial regulations, allowing rapid expansion of the financial sector. Asian competitors were beginning to put further pressure on companies competing in Western markets. The oil shock of 1973 and the start of recession and stagnation, including anaemic economic performance and persistently high inflation, offered conditions in which neoliberal ideas became a more attractive economic alternative to the consensus view. Uncertainty about the future of capitalism and the role of the state in relation to it created a new space for ideas on how to restructure the economic system, and its management. Neoliberal economic and political ideas spread more widely and came to the fore in an increasing number of public and political debates.

Within the context of the economic crisis, the solutions and arguments offered by neoliberal economists started to gain traction. They argued that markets were heavily constrained and that a more efficient allocation of resources, based on the price mechanism, would lead not only to economic growth but also to prices that better reflect people's preferences than the government could ever achieve. In the 1970s, the works of Hayek and Friedman received greater interest and influence within economics, culminating in Friedman's Nobel Prize in 1976. More support emerged for financial deregulation promoted by neoliberals because it removed restrictions on financial markets and private actors (especially corporations) who transacted in financial commodities. Growing support emerged for the idea that government are harming economies, and state intervention was not only reducing market efficiency but also threatening liberty. The neoliberal influence within the political domain was helped by the growing influence of think tanks and foundations such as the American Enterprise Institute, the Heritage Foundation in the United States, the Institute for Economic Affairs, and the Centre for Policy Studies in the UK. Across the Republican Party in the United States and the Conservative

Party in Britain, neoliberal ideas gained influence, and by the late 1970s and early 1980s resp. Margaret Thatcher and Ronald Reagan came to power; both were heavily influenced by neoliberal ideas and their administration are often seen as the zenith of neoliberalism in a political sense.

How to Understand Neoliberalism

The intellectual genealogy is somewhat transparent and orderly compared to how the concept of neoliberalism is understood and used outside the neoliberal intellectual canon outlined earlier. This undoubtedly has to do with the concept's popularity both within and outside academia. The usage of the concept has exploded in recent decades, and its meaning has been shaped more by its critics than by its proponents. Scholars and commentators have used the concept of neoliberalism in wide-ranging ways and within a growing number of debates within numerous academic and non-academic fields. The term is often undefined and used to characterise a wide variety of phenomena (Boas & Gans-Morse, 2009), often to express disapproval regarding a phenomenon or process. It therefore runs the risk of becoming what Flew (2014, p.49) calls an "all-purpose denunciatory category". Some highlight neoliberalism's unstable, partial, incoherent, heterogeneous, or even contradictory nature. Springer (2014, p.7) observes, "Neoliberalizing practices are thus understood as necessarily and always overdetermined, contingent, polymorphic, open to intervention, reconstituted, continually negotiated, impure, subject to counter-tendencies, and in a perpetual process of becoming".

We could start here with some general understanding, noting that neoliberalism materialises differently in different times and places (Ong, 2006; Peck & Tickell, 2002). A good but basic starting point could be Crouch (2011, p.7), for whom neoliberalism represents a fundamental preference for the market over the state as a means of resolving problems and achieving a human end. Mudge (2008, pp. 706–707) further clarifies that its "distinctive ideological core is the elevation of the market—understood as a non-political, non-cultural, machinelike entity" (p. 705) and that "[I]n all its modes, neo-liberalism is built on a single, fundamental principle: the superiority of individualised, market-based competition over other modes of organization" and—over all other modes of organisation (p. 705). To acknowledge its inherently disjointed nature as well as its influence of people's whole lifeworlds we can add Ball's definition of neoliberalism as a "complex, often incoherent, unstable and even contradictory set of practices that are organised around a certain imagination of 'the market' as a basis for the universalisation of market-based social relations, with the corresponding penetration in almost every single aspect of our lives" (2012, p. 18). Beyond this, we can distinguish three different versions of neoliberalism that are most useful in our analysis of the marketisation of HE drawn from existing analytical overviews of neoliberalism (e.g. Springer, 2012; Ward & England, 2007; Birch, 2015; Flew, 2014). These three approaches will inform the final three chapters of the book.

Neoliberalism as Policy

Neoliberal thinkers have extensively written about the role of the state, its limits, and its duties towards the legal order and the market. These ideas, alongside aligned economic theory, have been influential in developing and implementing government policy all over the world (Stedman Jones, 2012). From the 1970s onwards, when Keynesian economic models started to lose their appeal, Margaret Thatcher in the United Kingdom, Ronald Reagan in the United States, David Lange in New Zealand, Brian Mulroney in Canada, and Pinochet in Chile all experimented with neoliberal governance. In addition, the so-called 'Washington Consensus' is understood as a neoliberal economic programme by the World Bank, International Monetary Fund, and US Treasury of the late 1980s and early 1990s that affected many developing countries.

Neoliberal traces can be observed in many national government policies aimed at deregulation, privatisation, or promoting free trade agreements. For that reason, right-wing parties that traditionally have market-friendly policies have been called neoliberal. In some countries, such as the UK and the US, neoliberal ideas have arguably revolutionised politics itself, with durable commitment to neoliberal policies. Democrat Bill Clinton and New Labour's Tony Blair, who were critical of the more extreme positions of Reagan and Thatcher, have also been accused of being *essentially* neoliberal, introducing a policy mix of strong property rights, privatisation, free trade, market liberalisation, deregulation, and national competitiveness. Other social-democratic and corporatist countries we do not normally associate with neoliberalism have adopted measures that potentially fit the neoliberal policy paradigm. Given the widespread policy changes that can be described as neoliberalism, we immediately see the difficulties in pinning down the self-contained neoliberal policy blueprint, or who the neoliberal political actors are/were.

If we want to use neoliberalism as a policy approach, we need to acknowledge this lack of clear demarcation, particularly towards other free or pro-market initiatives. It also takes different forms but, at a minimum, remains directed or inspired by neoliberal ideas about the role of the state and market in the conceptualisation, delivery, and implementation of government policy at various levels. As it is not always easy to distinguish neoliberal policies from other free marketeer initiatives, it is equally difficult to pinpoint how neoliberalism manifests within policy, as again, evidence of neoliberal policies can be found throughout Western post-war policies. Neoliberalism is a difficult concept to define and open to interpretation. For instance, Brown (2015, p. 28) adopts a much wider than usual set of examples of neoliberal policy that include wider capitalist and social change, ranging from replacing progressive with regressive tax and tariff schemes to privatised and outsourced public goods and a radical reduction in welfare state provision. Here, we could point to the drive to expand any policies that actively promote the market in all areas of life.

For many political scientists neoliberal ideas seem to have been an important driver of government policy. Blyth (2005 as cited by Peck, 2008, p. 32) noted that "neoliberalism remains the "dominant prism through which policymakers understand the world, the ideational matrix through which contemporary policy 'problems' are comprehended, and responses framed". Others remain less convinced (e.g. Peck, 2013). In particular, outside the Anglo-Saxon world, its influence is questioned and implemented with significant compromise and experimentation in practice. Evans and Sewell (2013, p. 41) observed

> *[B]ecause the United States was the world's hegemonic power, its turn to neoliberalism in the early 1980s put the issue of neoliberal reforms on the political agenda in all the noncommunist countries—which were all, in any case, searching for policies that might lift them out of the era's extended economic crisis. In fact, most politicians in the advanced capitalist powers remained quite skeptical of Thatcher's and Reagan's ideological zeal.*

No national policy can be close to being a 'pure' neoliberalist, and so the influence of neoliberalism on the development and implementation of policies is partial and, therefore, hard to distinguish from other policy drivers. Also, neoliberal policies have been implemented in different ways and in vastly different national contexts creating many hybrids. Peck et al. (2018, p. 3) emphasise the "cumulative and combinatorial character of neoliberalization" produced by "checkered, uneven, and variegated realities of those governing schemes and restructuring programs variously enacted in the name of competition, choice, freedom, and efficiency". Yet for the purpose of this book, we need to have a working definition of policies and agendas we can name as neoliberal, without finding a pure form. We can understand neoliberalism as a policy programme aiming to extend markets through protection and advancements of private property and free market mechanisms, transfer of ownership from the state to the private sector or corporate interests that include privatisation (see Brenner & Theodore, 2002; Klepeis & Vance, 2003; Steger & Roy, 2010). Additionally, we could include a general hostility towards the welfare state, regulation, and full-employment policies. Deregulation is also often mentioned as a neoliberal policy aim, yet 'deregulation' is far less of a goal in itself. Only deregulation that improves the functioning of the free market is acceptable.

Yet crucially, as explained earlier, the state's role within neoliberalism is, at least in a Hayekian sense, active, in contrast to the liberal night watchman state in its classical conceptualisation, where a minimal state takes on a non-interventionist approach as far as possible. Amable (2011, p. 17) explained that a neoliberal state is one *"that establishes and preserves, through its constant action [...], a competitive market order which is an artificial human creation and not a product of nature"*. The state must be an active force and cannot simply rely on 'market forces'. We can observe both an attack on the state and its perceived propensity to limit freedom and the free market. At the same time, there is a recognition of the need for a strong state that can create the institutions necessary to maintain a free market (e.g. Buchanan, 1986; Hayek, 1944). The ideal would be a strong interventionist state that can impose policy reform based on neoliberal principles.

The 1990s are often seen as the pinnacle of neoliberal dominance, and some have voiced that neoliberal state governance is now over (e.g. Matutinovic, 2020). In particular, the financial crisis of 2008 and its deep recession made some think that neoliberalism has shown its flaws, especially around financialisation, expanding risk calculus into non-productive areas of social life, which can then be drawn into the financial economy. A neoliberal state seems to underwrite the financial sector, privatising gains and socialising the losses (Krippner, 2011). Yet others, such as Mirowski (2013), argued that the financial crisis was an opportunity to insert neoliberalism policies. Davies and Gane (2021, p. 16) suggested that the

COVID-19 pandemic also led to "a more dramatic overturning of neoliberal orthodoxies than any other financial or political crises of the previous two decades".

Some have argued that neoliberalist policy forces have not disappeared, but have shifted. Craig and Cotterell (2007) distinguished between the first and second phases of neoliberal policy. In the first phase, social and institutional arrangements were broken down and subjected to a market regime. The second phase would try to sustain the position of the free market while ameliorating some of the extreme social effects of the market. In the British context, New Labour is often seen as an example of the second phase of neoliberal political force, in which market fundamentalism remained and added what Hall calls "managerial marketisation" (Hall, 2011, p. 19). Others have highlighted that neoliberalism as a policy force is at odds with democracy and see democratic deterioration as an ongoing outcome of neoliberalisation. The anti-democratic nature of neoliberalism lies in the power transfer between state and market, eliminating politics from public life. For this reason, Heller (2016) labels neoliberalism 'authoritarian liberalism'.

Neoliberalism as Ideology

A second approach to understanding neoliberalism is to define it as a capitalist ideology. According to Harvey (2005, pp. 19–20), the objective of neoliberalism is the fulfilment of economic liberty. We can see this goal achieved through ideological means that shape and change minds throughout society. Neoliberalism then becomes a taken-for-granted rationality that disseminates "the model of the market to all domains and activities" to configure "human beings exhaustively as market actors, always, only, and everywhere as *Homo oeconomicus*" (Brown, 2015, p. 31; see also Gilbert, 2013; Hall et al., 2013; Schram, 2015). Expanding this economic rationality into cultural, political, and social spheres is a powerful ideological tool to support the interest of capital.

The concept of ideology can describe a wide range of phenomena. Eagleton (1991) discerned various understandings of ideology by identifying the following six theoretical approaches:

1. Ideology as the "production of ideas, beliefs, and values in social life" (= ideology as culture) (p. 28); 2. Ideas and beliefs of "a specific, socially significant group or class" (29) (= ideology as worldview) (p. 29); 3. The "*promotion* and *legitimation* of the interests" of a group "in the face of

opposing interests" (p. 29); 4. The "promotion and legitimation of sectoral interests" in the "activities of a dominant social power" (= ideology as dominant worldviews) (p. 29); 5. "[I]deas and beliefs which help to legitimate the interests of a ruling group or class specifically by distortion and dissimulation" (p. 30); 6. "[F]alse or deceptive beliefs [...] arising not from the interests of a dominant class but from the material structure of society as a whole" (p. 30). The second, third, fourth, and fifth, in particular, can be used in positioning neoliberalism as an ideology. An ideology within this framework tends to see ideology as a perspective on reality (a way of looking at things), cultivated through certain belief systems and morals in society and can dominate the social thinking of social groups and populations (Klikauer, 2013).

Within a Marxist framework, ideologies function to reproduce and expand their material existence, maintained through powerful superstructures in society (which include the state, religion, and the media). Ideology prevents people from understanding a complex reality, as it legitimises both the means and goals it advocates. For neoliberalism to be an ideology, we can think of neoliberal ideology as a culture in which the need for market and competition become part of our understanding of the world (McGuigan, 2016).

For many authors in the neoliberalism-as-ideology approach, neoliberalism is a doctrine that started as an intellectual movement linked to the members of the Mont Pèlerin Society, such as Hayek, as discussed earlier (Mirowski & Plehwe, 2009). Their ideas have been popularised and used directly through political actors with the help of think tanks, networks, and foundations (e.g. Institute of Economic Affairs, the Atlas Economic Research Foundation, the Heritage Foundation, and the American Legislative Exchange Council), ultimately leading to mainstream acceptance. Equally important are supranational bodies that became globally imposed and accepted through the work of the IMF and World Bank and the so-called Washington Consensus that imposed their neoliberal policies and ideas on other countries.

Neoliberalism as an ideology is, of course, connected to neoliberalism as a policy domain. Since the elections of Thatcher and Reagan, we can see clear societal changes in the UK and the US, respectively (Jackson & Saunders, 2012; Gerstle, 2022), and their time in office allowed capitalism to have a greater grip over citizens and forces such as think tanks and lobby groups to take a firmer grip over civil society. This tight relationship with capitalist power makes neoliberalism a distinct ideology. Neoliberalism is presented as an attempt to restore the power of the capitalist class power that was lost. Slobodian (2018) argued that neoliberalism attempts to protect global capitalism from its own contradictions and external shocks and to reduce the impact of democratic decision making and protect the interests of capital. Through a belief system with explicit assumptions about the role of the free market in society, it actively delegitimises any alternatives as not viable or possible. As a result, class and power inequalities are obscured. Through their power over cultural, media, and state institutions, support and consent for free-market policies is assured within the neoliberal society (Duménil & Lévy, 2004; Harvey, 2005; Plehwe et al., 2006). According to Schram (2015, p. 25), neoliberalism has blurred the boundaries between market, state, and civil society, making neoliberalism 'the new normal'.

Closely linked to neoliberalism as ideology is "market fundamentalism" (Block & Somers, 2014), which refers to a quasi-religious faith in the power of markets to secure efficient outcomes and a strong denunciation of the idea that states could allocate resources efficiently and should not intervene in the economy. In addition, the neoliberal association between market rule and liberal freedoms builds on a utilitarian conception of market rationality and competitive individualism. These ultimately aid capitalism and benefit the ruling class. As a result, governments introduced markets in the delivery of the public sector (Blyth, 2002; Prasad, 2006). They have individualised social problems, rejecting earlier goals of social redistribution and solidarity. Citizens are thought to be empowered to improve their own lives without relying on government social provision, adhering to the idea that "human well-being can best be advanced by liberating individual entrepreneurial freedoms and skills within an institutional framework characterized by strong property rights, free markets and free trade" (Harvey, 2005, p. 2).

Neo-marxist authors, perhaps unsurprisingly, have made the largest contribution to this conceptualisation of neoliberalism, drawing on wider 'dominant ideology' theories. The most influential authors and proponents of the ideological understanding of neoliberalism are arguably Chomsky (1998), Harvey (2005), Smart (2003), Stiglitz (2002), and Klein (2007). Marx explains how those with the means of production also have "control over the means of mental production, so that thereby, generally speaking, those who lack the means of mental production are subject to it" (Marx & Engels, 1970, p. 64). Through a 'bourgeois ideology', the ruling class, who has an interest in presenting its own interests as though they were universal, misled the working classes. The misrepresentation of the actual material conditions of society creates a false consciousness serving capitalist interests. Marx's ideas have been further developed by Gramsci and Lukács and the Frankfurt School in various ways (Feenberg, 2014). They further demonstrated that the dominant ideology in bourgeois society misrepresents social relations in ways that legitimise the capitalist exploitation of the masses. Neoliberalism as an ideological approach continues this way of thinking (Harvey, 2005; Overbeek & van Apeldoorn, 2012; Duménil & Lévy, 2011). The neoliberal *political* hegemonic project can restore and "re-establish the conditions for capital accumulation and restore economic elites' power" (Harvey, 2005, p. 19). Neo-marxist accounts often highlight its global dimension, as the US-led political free-market ideology dominates the post-communist and developing world. Global economic elites propagate false ideas to maintain class power and enrol the whole population into a world order in which "some lives, if not whole groups, are seen as disposable and redundant" (Giroux, 2008, p. 594).

The strong version of the interpretation of neoliberalism as hegemony has lost its popularity. It has faced various criticisms, such as whether this perspective allows for enough agency to capture ongoing resistance. Cultural theorist Stuart Hall (1988), when writing about the hegemonic project of Thatcherism, clearly identified the contestation and struggle by those subjected to it. Instead of assuming acquiescence by a uniform neoliberal discourse, individuals offer contrasting claims and negotiated understandings of the world as well as their identities in response to it (Hall, 2011; see also Abercrombie & Turner, 1978). The problem with neoliberalism as an ideology is that, similar to neoliberalism as policy, the ideology always exists with other ideologies and can never be fully hegemonic. For Hall, neoliberal hegemony is always partial, never permanent, "a process, not a state of being [...] constantly to be 'worked on', maintained, renewed, and revised" (Hall, 2011, p. 26).

Neo-liberalism as Governmentality: Production of Neoliberal Subjectivity

A third version of neoliberalism presents it as a force that (re)constructs power and wealth throughout the world (although some consider neoliberalism more as a *discourse* through which a political-economic form of power-knowledge is constructed, e.g. Springer, 2016). Central is the idea that neoliberalism has led to more rather than less governance. Despite its repudiation of the state, it has led to forms of governance through the state that encourage institutions and individuals to conform to market norms. It highlights how neoliberalism uses distinct technologies by which populations are governed through regimes of truth and the formation of new subjectivities required by market discourse.

Foucault and Governmentality
This account of neoliberalism draws explicitly on the work of philosopher Michel Foucault in general, his writing on neoliberalism, and his analysis of the underlying governmentalities. Foucault observed the historical emergence of distinctive types of rule, which focused on the conduct of individuals or groups and how it can be directed (Foucault, 1978, 2008; see also Gane, 2008; Flew, 2012). In the modern model of governmentality, power is embedded in discourses or systems of knowledge. Discourses regulate human relationships; power does not belong to certain agents or institutions. "*To govern is to control the possible field of action of others*" (Foucault, 1994, p. 341). The traditional model of government is based on the state, which is central to the sovereignty of government power (associated with Machiavelli and Hobbes). Power was predominantly a negative force, used to be expressed through coercion (Foucault, 1977, 1981; Clegg et al., 2006).

The emphasis in governmentality is not to coerce or repress populations but to actively use and exploit them to maintain power and to govern. This means that the state does not govern centrally but rather through actors and institutions across society via the functioning of discourses. The new mode of governmentality is based on and legitimated by systems of knowledge or discourses rather than a sovereign force (Hindess, 1996). Through the introduction or imposition of new discourses—new mentalities—subjects take themselves up as the newly appropriate and appropriated subjects of the new social order.

The state is no longer a "unified entity that can be 'captured' by competing political groups" (Flew, 2014, p. 61). Instead, power is expressed with the consent of the governed. Governance becomes the 'conduct of conduct', directing or guiding subjects' thinking, actions, and emotions to achieve a desired set of behaviours. Its success depends on the ability of citizens to govern themselves, setting out the conditions under which they are enabled to do so through a diffuse array of techniques. Each mode of governmentality promotes specific rationalities (ways of knowing) by furthering specific mentalities (ways of thinking), which inform particular types of government and foster specific human conduct (Dean, 1999; Foucault, 1981; Rose, 1999).

Foucault and Neoliberalism

Foucault drew upon the concept of neoliberalism to analyse forms of governance and the constitution of a particular type of market subject that neoliberal discourse envisions (Dean, 1999, 2007; O'Malley, 1992; Rose, 1999; Skålén, 2009, 2010). Foucault's ideas on neoliberalism are most clearly expressed in the series of lectures presented by Foucault at the College de France in 1978–1979 (Foucault, 2008). A subsequent large literature is dedicated to discussing Foucault's understanding of neoliberal governmentality (see Gane, 2008; Tribe, 2009; Behrent, 2009). There is considerable debate about how Foucault understands neoliberalism (see Dean, 2018). Foucault offers a genealogy of liberal thought, leading into a history of neoliberalism up to that point. Classic liberalism as adopted in nineteenth-century laissez-faire Britain demonstrated the market's natural legitimacy or self-evident efficiency. Neoliberalism is not a rerun of classical liberalism and actively promotes market-enabling and market-conforming economic policies. Whereas classical liberalism highlights the natural efficiency of markets, which is served by refraining from intervention, neoliberalism holds that there is nothing natural about the market and because of this, markets cannot simply be left to their own devices. Instead, they must be tied to the government. For Foucault, neoliberalism serves as an approach to governing and views the market or economic order as simultaneously natural and cultivated.

Neoliberalism is a form of *statecraft* that uses practical and technical techniques to govern states (Peck & Theodore, 2015; Foucault, 2008). Neoliberalism relies on a market-based governmentality using discourses and technologies outside and inside the state to produce subjects that are individualised, disciplined, and entrepreneurial. The market offers the basis for the legitimation of the state. The state's role is to serve the market's interest, and it can only be used to protect its freedom. The market produces the legitimacy of the state, and the market economy should be the principle of the state's "internal regulation from start to finish of its existence and action" (Foucault, 2008, p. 116). It is a state "under the supervision of the market rather than a market supervised by the state" (Foucault, 2008, p. 116). Rather than the state ensuring the legitimacy of the market, it is the market that produces legitimacy for the state, which in turn becomes its 'guarantor'. The free market becomes the organising and regulating principle of the state. The market economy serves as the "principle, form, and model" of the state (Gane, 2012, p. 626). This means that neoliberalism's governmentality disconnects the government from the state. The population becomes a resource to be economically exploited through marketisation (Dean, 1995, 1999).

Neoliberal Subjectivity
Foucauldian scholars argue that neoliberalism can be understood as a 'mentality of governing' (Rose, 1996) which 'engineers' the free subject (Burchell, 1996). Neoliberalism, as a force of governmentality, shapes the individual through its discourse, leading to various forms of self-monitoring and self-discipline. Individuals express their freedom through self-governance, which is in line with the market subjectivity that neoliberal discourse espouses, namely, as active, entrepreneurial, and responsible individuals. For Foucault, the subject moves away from the classic liberal version of *Homo oeconomicus*, who, through exchange, acts according to their utility and needs in a market of producers or consumers (Foucault, 2008, p. 225). Rather, *Homo oeconomicus* is "an entrepreneur, an entrepreneur of himself" (Foucault, 2008, p. 226) who "will maximise its own human capital, project itself a future and seek to shape itself in order to become that it wishes to be".

The new *Homo oeconomicus* is extremely governable. Neoliberal governance is exercised in a distant yet all-pervasive manner—the whole experience of subjects. Subjects are ordered to maximise their potential for individual happiness and success, always striving towards set goals through continual self-improvement and continuously acting on the environment. Technologies of the self are practices used by individuals in constructing their own selves which "permit individuals to effect by their own means, or with the help of others, a certain number of operations on their own bodies and souls, thoughts, conduct, and way of being, so as to transform themselves in order to attain a certain state of happiness, purity, wisdom, perfection, or immortality" (Foucault, 1988, p. 18). Neoliberalisation draws on a subjectification process that creates autonomous, choosing, self-managing and self-improving subjects whose value is expressed in market terms.

Neoliberal governmentality has a special relationship with risk. According to Rose (1993, p. 269), the collectivised risk-taking associated with the welfare society is replaced with individual responsibilisation or "privatisation of risk management". Self-interested market orientation to risk is applied throughout people's lives, including education, health, and welfare. The 'passive' citizens of the welfare state become active, responsible actors expressing themselves through calculated acts and investments. Through the moral valuation of self-reliance and self-advancement, it does away with previous valuations of collective responsibility for the vulnerable and marginalised.

Neoliberal Discourse

Understanding neoliberalism as governmentality in practice is closely related to understanding it as discourse, although the latter is not necessarily linked to Foucault's work (Springer, 2012). For Foucault, self-government involves a subject guided by discourses, shaped by their understanding of what is right and wrong, and orients themselves towards a particular subjectivity. Generally, a discourse regulates behaviour within a particular institutional or societal context by giving meaning and determining what and what not can be said (Laclau & Mouffe, 1985). Thus, a discourse is performative, as it describes and shapes the social world (in particular, in post-structural theory, 'the social' and 'the self' are mutually constituted through discourse). For neoliberalism, this means that we are looking for "rearticulations and representations of neoliberal discourse in the form of particular discourses of neoliberalization, where individual actors take a proactive role in reshaping the formal practices of politics, policy, and administration" (Springer, 2012, p. 142). Neoliberal discourses are underpinned by economic and market-driven changes in how society are represented in the public realm previously not characterised by economic relations (Crouch, 2011; Touraine, 2001). Some have used the concept of discourse to illuminate the neoliberal influence on the policy landscape. Through those changes and shifts, neoliberalism has altered our common sense, how we understand, interpret, and talk about the world, and how we can change it. As such, it becomes "hegemonic as a mode of discourse" (Harvey, 2005, p. 3).

CONCLUSION

In the second part of this chapter, we saw significant differences and similarities between the three main neoliberal approaches. Some key neoliberal axioms are as follows:

- Government intervention in the market is harmful; it disrupts the natural equilibrium of supply and demand.

- Value of markets. The price system is invaluable, unique, and irreplaceable, as it is a fast and efficient method of supplying information on consumer demand to which producers and providers will respond.
- Expressions of human subjectivity are meaningless without ratification by the market.
- Society could only be truly free if it had economic freedom.
- The state should be in the service of the market. The market is democratic and offers efficient solutions to social and policy problems.

So, how can we use neoliberalism to make sense of marketisation in HE? There are considerable differences within neoliberalism. How neoliberalism has shaped the world is partial and uneven and cannot be easily understood. The second part of the chapter offers three broad approaches that could illuminate different dimensions of marketisation. Treating these as ideal types is essential because, in practice, they can overlap. Each of the three understandings is used simultaneously or taken together. We can use the three approaches as heuristic devices and analyse the marketisation phenomenon. The three approaches are summarised below (Table 3.1):

Table 3.1 Three approaches to neoliberalism

	Focus	Role of the state	Role of the market and competition
Neoliberalism as policy	Government policy on all levels of stakeholders	Key actor in developing and implementing neoliberal policy	Policy is created, implemented and enforced to facilitate the markets and expand their influence on society
Neoliberalism as ideology	Shaping and changing minds throughout society	Important conduit of neoliberal ideology	Market fundamentalism: Markets need the faith of people for capitalism to function and disguise unequal power relations
Neoliberalism as subjectivity	Modes of governmentality	Neoliberalism governs states (statecraft) with its own practical and technical techniques, including discourses and technologies outside and inside the state	Market-based governmentality: Subject's values are self-expressed in market terms; the ethos of competitiveness permeates not just the government but also culture, education, personal relations, and orientation to the self

References

Abercrombie, N., & Turner, B. (1978). The dominant ideology thesis. *British Journal of Sociology*, 29(2), 149–170.
Amable, B. (2011). Morals and politics in the ideology of neo-liberalism. *Socio-Economic Review*, 9(1), 3–30.
Ball, S. J. (2012). Performativity, commodification, and commitment: An I-Spy guide to the neoliberal university. *British Journal of Educational Studies*, 60(1), 17–28.
Becker, G. S. (1990). *The Economic Approach to Human Behavior*. Chicago University Press.
Behrent, M. (2009). Liberalism without humanism: Michel Foucault and the free market creed 1976–1979. *Modern Intellectual History*, 6(3), 539–568.
Biebricher, T. (2018). *The Political Theory of Neoliberalism*. Stanford University Press.
Birch, K. (2015). *We Have Never Been Neoliberal*. Zero Books.
Block, F., & Somers, M. R. (2014). *The Power of Market Fundamentalism: Karl Polanyi's Critique*. Harvard University.
Blyth, M. (2002). *Great Transformations: Economic Ideas and Institutional Change in the Twentieth Century*. Cambridge University Press.
Boas, T. C., & Gans-Morse, J. (2009). Neoliberalism: From new liberal philosophy to anti-liberal slogan. *Studies in Comparative International Development*, 44(2), 137–161.
Brenner, N., & Theodore, N. (Eds.). (2002). *Spaces of Neoliberalism: Urban Restructuring in North America and Western Europe*. Blackwell.
Brown, W. (2015). *Undoing the Demos: Neoliberalism's Stealth Revolution*. Zone Books.
Buchanan, J. M. (1975). *The Limits of Liberty: Between Anarchy and Leviathan*. Chicago University of Chicago Press.
Buchanan, J. M. (1986). *Liberty, Market and State*. New York University Press.
Buchanan, J., Wagner, M., Richard, E., & Burton, J. (1978). *The Consequences of Mr. Keynes*. Institute of Economic Affairs.
Burchell, G. (1996). Liberal government and techniques of the self. In A. Barry, T. Osborne, & N. Rose (Eds.), *Foucault and Political Reason* (pp. 19–36). University of Chicago Press.
Burgin, A. (2012). *The Great Persuasion: Reinventing Free Markets since the Depression*. Harvard University Press.
Caldwell, B. (2004). *Hayek's Challenge: An Intellectual Biography of F.A. Hayek*. University of Chicago Press.
Chang, H.-J. (2002). Breaking the mould: An institutionalist political economy alternative to the neo-liberal theory of the market and the state. *Cambridge Journal of Economics*, 26(5), 539–559.
Chomsky, N. (1998). *Profit over People: Neoliberalism and Global Order*. Seven Stories Press.

Clegg, S. R., Courpasson, D., & Phillips, N. (2006). *Power and Organizations*. Sage.
Craig, D., & Cotterell, G. (2007). Periodising neoliberalism? *Policy & Politics*, 35(3), 497–514.
Crouch, C. (2011). *The Strange Non-Death of Neoliberalism*. Polity Press.
Davies, W., & Gane, N. (2021). Post-Neoliberalism? An introduction. *Theory, Culture & Society*, 38(6), 3–28.
Dean, M. (1995). Governing the unemployed self in an active society. *Economy and Society*, 24(4), 559–583.
Dean, M. (1999). *Governmentality: Power and Rule in Modern Society*. Sage.
Dean, M. (2007). *Governing Societies: Political Perspectives on Domestic and International Rule*. Open University Press.
Dean, M. (2018). Foucault and the neoliberalism controversy. In D. Cahill, M. Cooper, M. Konings, & D. Primrose (Eds.), *The Sage Handbook of Neoliberalism* (pp. 40–53). Sage.
Duménil, G., & Lévy, D. (2004). *Capital Resurgent: Roots of the Neoliberal Revolution*. Harvard University Press.
Duménil, G., & Levy, D. (2011). *The Crisis of Neoliberalism*. Harvard University Press.
Eagleton, T. (1991). *Ideology: An Introduction*. Verso books.
Evans, P., & Sewell, W. H. (2013). Neoliberalism: Policy regimes, international regimes, and social effects. In P. Hall & M. Lamont (Eds.), *Social Resilience in the Neoliberal Era* (pp. 35–68). Cambridge University Press.
Feenberg, A. (2014). *The Philosophy of Praxis: Marx, Lukács and the Frankfurt School*. Verso books.
Feser, E. (Ed.). (2006). *Cambridge Companion to Hayek Cambridge*. Cambridge University press.
Flew, T. (2012). Michel Foucault's the birth of biopoliitcs and contemporary neoliberalism debates. *Thesis Eleven*, 108(1), 47–65.
Flew, T. (2014). Six theories of neoliberalism. *Thesis Eleven*, 122(1), 49–71.
Foucault, M. (1977). *Discipline and Punish: The Birth of the Prison*. Penguin.
Foucault, M. (1978). *The History of Sexuality Volume 1: An Introduction* (R. Hurley, Trans.). Pantheon Books.
Foucault, M. (1981). *The Will to Knowledge: The History of Sexuality* (Vol. 1). Penguin.
Foucault, M. (1988). Technologies of the self. In L. H. Martin, H. Gutman, & P. H. Hutton (Eds.), *Technologies of the Self* (pp. 16–49). University of Massachusetts Press.
Foucault, M. (1994). The subject and power. In J. D. Faubion (Ed.), *Michel Foucault – Power: The essential works of Foucault* (Vol. 3, pp. 327–348). Penguin.
Foucault, M. (2008). *The Birth of Biopolitics: Lectures at the Collège de France, 1978–79*. Palgrave.
Friedman, M. (1962). *Capitalism and Freedom*. University of Chicago Press.

Gane, M. (2008). Foucault on governmentality and liberalism. *Theory, Culture & Society*, 25(7–8), 353–363.
Gane, N. (2012). The governmentalities of neoliberalism: Panopticism, post-panopticism and beyond. *The Sociological Review*, 60(4), 611–634.
Gerstle, G. (2022). *The Rise and Fall of the Neoliberal Order: America and the World in the Free Market Era*. Oxford University Press.
Gilbert, J. (2013). What kind of thing is "Neoliberalism"? new formations. *A Journal of Culture/Theory/Politics*, 80(80), 7–22.
Giroux, H. A. (2008). Beyond Biopolitics of disposability: Rethinking neoliberalism in the New Gilded Age. *Social Identities*, 14(5), 587–620.
Hall, S. (1988). *Thatcherism and the Crisis of the Left: The Hard Road to Renewal*. Verso.
Hall, S. (2011). The neoliberal revolution. *Soundings*, 48, 9–28.
Hall, S., Massey, D., & D. and M. Rustin, M. (2013). After neoliberalism: Analysing the present. *Soundings*, 53, 8–22.
Harvey, D. A. (2005). *Brief History of Neoliberalism*. Oxford University Press.
Hayek, F. A. (1944). *The Road to Serfdom*. Routledge & Kegan Paul.
Hayek, F. A. (1948). *Individualism and Economic Order*. University of Chicago Press.
Hayek, F. A. (1945). The use of knowledge in society. *American Economic Review*, 35(4), 519–530.
Hayek, F. A. (1967). *Studies in Philosophy, Politics and Economics*. Routledge.
Hayek, F. A. (1973). *Law, Legislation & Liberty, Volume 1: Rules and Order*. Routledge & Kegan Paul.
Hayek, F. A. (1976). *Law, Legislation and Liberty, Volume 2: The Mirage of Social Justice*. Routledge & Kegan Paul.
Hayek, F. A. (2002). Competition as a discovery procedure. *Quarterly Journal of Austrian Economics*, 5(3), 9–23.
Hayek, F. A. (2006). *The Constitution of Liberty*. Routledge.
Heller, H. (2016). *The Capitalist University: The Transformations of Higher Education in the United States Since 1945*. Pluto Press.
Hindess, B. (1996). *Discourses of Power: From Hobbes to Foucault*. Blackwell.
Jackson, B., & Saunders, R. (2012). *Making Thatcher's Britain*. Cambridge University Press.
Kiely, R. (2018). *The Neoliberal Paradox*. Edward Elgar.
Klein, N. (2007). *The Shock Doctrine: The Rise of Disaster Capitalism*. Metropolitan Books/Henry Holt.
Klepeis, P., & Vance, C. (2003). Neoliberal policy and deforestation in Southeastern Mexico: An assessment of the PROCAMPO program. *Economic Geography*, 79(3), 221–240.
Klikauer, T. (2013). *Managerialism: A Critique of an Ideology*. Palgrave Macmillan.
Krippner, G. (2011). *Capitalizing on Crisis: The Political Origins of the Rise of Finance*. Harvard University Press.

Laclau, E., & Mouffe, C. (1985). *Hegemony and socialist strategy: towards a radical democratic politics* (2nd ed.). Verso books.
Marx, K., & Engels, F. (1970). *The German Ideology: Part One*. International Publishers.
Matutinovic, I. (2020). The end of neoliberal ideology. *Green European Journal*. Retrieved April 24, 2024, from https://www.greeneuropeanjournal.eu/the-end-of-neoliberal-ideology/
McGuigan, J. (2016). *Neoliberal Culture*. Palgrave Macmillan.
Mirowski, P. (2013). *Never Let a Serious Crisis Go to Waste: How Neoliberalism Survived the Financial Meltdown*. Verso books.
Mirowski, P., Plehwe, D., & D. (2009). *The Road from Mont Pèlerin: The Making of the Neoliberal Thought Collective*. Harvard University Press.
Mises, von, L. (2007). *Human Action*. Liberty Fund.
Mudge, S. L. (2008). The state of the art: What is neo-liberalism? *Socio-Economic Review, 6*(4), 703–731.
Nik-Khah, E., van Horn, R., & R. (2016). The ascendancy of Chicago neoliberalism. In S. Springer, K. Birch, & J. MacLeavy (Eds.), *The Handbook of Neoliberalism* (pp. 27–38). Routledge.
O'Malley, P. (1992). Risk, power and crime prevention. *Economy & Society, 21*(3), 252–275.
Ong, A. (2006). *Neoliberalism as Exception: Mutations in Citizenship and Sovereignty*. Duke University Press.
Overbeek, H., & Van Apeldoorn, B. (2012). *Neoliberalism in Crisis*. Palgrave Macmillan.
Peck, J. (2008). Remaking laissez-faire. *Progress in Human Geography, 32*(1), 3–43.
Peck, J. (2013). Explaining (with) neoliberalism. *Territory, Politics, Governance, 1*(2), 132–157.
Peck, J., Brenner, N., & Theodore, N. (2018). Actually existing neoliberalism. In D. Cahill, M. Cooper, M. Konings, & D. Primrose (Eds.), *The Sage Handbook of Neoliberalism* (pp. 3–15). Sage.
Peck, J., & Theodore, N. (2015). *Fast Policy: Experimental Statecraft at the Thresholds of Neoliberalism*. University of Minnesota Press.
Peck, J., & Tickell, T. A. (2002). Neoliberalizing space. *Antipode, 34*(3), 380–404.
Plehwe, D., Walpen, B., & Neunhoffer, G. (2006). Introduction: Reconsidering neoliberal hegemony. In D. Plehwe, B. Walpen, & G. Neunhoffer (Eds.), *Neoliberal Hegemony: A Global Critique* (pp. 1–24). Routledge.
Prasad, M. (2006). *The Politics of Free Markets: The Rise of Neoliberal Economic Policies in Britain, France, Germany and the United States*. University of Chigago.
Rose, N. (1993). Government, authority and expertise in advanced liberalism. *Economy & Society, 22*(3), 283–299.
Rose, N. (1996). *Inventing Our Selves*. Cambridge University Press.

Rose, N. (1999). *Powers of Freedom: Reframing Political Thought*. Cambridge University Press.
Schmidt, V. (2018). Ideas and the rise of neoliberalism in Europe. In D. Cahill, M. Cooper, M. Konings, & D. Primrose (Eds.), *The Sage Handbook of Neoliberalism* (pp. 69–81). Sage.
Schram, S. (2015). *The Return of Ordinary Capitalism: Neoliberalism, Precarity, Occupy*. Oxford University Press.
Skålén, P. (2009). Service marketing and subjectivity: The shaping of customer-oriented proactive employees. *Journal of Marketing Management*, 25(7–8), 795–809.
Skålén, P. (2010). *Managing Service Firms: The Power of Managerial Marketing*. Routledge.
Slobodian, Q. (2018). *Globalists: The End of Empire and the Birth of Neoliberalism*. Harvard University Press.
Smart, B. (2003). *Economy, Culture and Society: A Sociological Critique of Neoliberalism*. Open University Press.
Springer, S. (2012). Neoliberalism as discourse: Between Foucauldian political economy and Marxian poststructuralism. *Critical Discourse Studies*, 9(2), 133–147.
Springer, S. (2014). Postneoliberalism? *Review of Radical Political Economics*, 47(1), 5–17.
Springer, S. (2016). *The Discourse of Neoliberalism: An Anatomy of a Powerful Idea*. Rowman and Littlefield.
Stedman Jones, D. (2012). *Masters of the Universe: Hayek, Friedman, and the Birth of Neoliberal Politics*. Princeton University Press.
Steger, M. B., & Roy, R. K. (2010). *Neoliberalism: A Very Short Introduction*. Oxford University Press.
Stiglitz, J. E. (2002). *Globalization and its Discontents*. Allen Lane/Penguin.
Touraine, A. (2001). *Beyond Neoliberalism*. Polity.
Tribe, K. (2009). The political economy of modernity: Foucault's College de France lectures of 1978 and 1979. *Economy and Society*, 38(4), 679–698.
Tullock, G. (1967). The welfare costs of tariffs, monopolies, and theft. *Western Economic Journal*, 5, 224–232.
Van Horn, R., Mirowski, P., & Stapleford, T. A. (Eds.). (2013). *Building Chicago Economics: New Perspectives on the History of America's Most Powerful Economics Program*. Cambridge University Press.
Ward, K., & England, K. (2007). Introduction: Reading neoliberalization. In K. England & K. Ward (Eds.), *Neoliberalization: States, Networks, People* (pp. 1–22). Blackwell.

CHAPTER 4

How Has Neoliberalism Been Applied to HE?

Abstract This chapter examines how the concept of neoliberalism has been used in the academic literature on HE. It demonstrates that in the field of education, neoliberalism is used to critique a range of processes and practices in and management of the HE sector or specifically (public) universities. The chapter then demonstrates how all three approaches of neoliberalism outlined in Chap. 3 can be applied to comprehend how HE and universities have changed over time.

Keywords Neoliberalism • Higher Education • Policy • Ideology • Governmentality

Arguably more than any other type of education, neoliberalism is used as a heuristic device to demonstrate the changes in HE dominance of neoliberalism (e.g. Hill, 2003; Kezar, 2004; Levidow, 2005; McLaren, 2005; Slaughter & Rhoades, 2004). This chapter analyses how the concept of neoliberalism has been associated with HE in the scholarly literature. Given the size of the literature, I will cover some key areas in which neoliberalism has emerged as a popular concept that explains and typifies the state of HE.

© The Author(s), under exclusive license to Springer Nature Switzerland AG 2024
G. Tholen, *The Role of Neoliberalism in the Marketisation of Higher Education*, Palgrave Studies on Global Policy and Critical Futures in Education, https://doi.org/10.1007/978-3-031-66281-2_4

Neoliberal thinkers throughout have identified education as an area where the free market could blossom but were often restricted or curtailed by governments. Hayek (2006) argued that education should not be controlled by the state but should be left to individuals and private institutions to provide. The state only has to ensure that all children have access to education and that there are minimum standards of quality and safety. Emphasising the importance of individual freedom and decentralised decision making, offering freedom to choose is the state's main mission for its involvement in education. Parents and communities should be free to choose the educational institutions and programmes that best suit their needs and values. Hayek believed that individuals were best suited to make decisions about their own education because they knew their own needs and interests better than anyone else. He also believed that competition among educational providers would lead to greater efficiency and innovation in the education sector, ultimately benefiting students and society as a whole. The quality of education would be improved through school choice, vouchers, and for-profit education markets.

A 1955 essay by Friedman on the role of government in education is often seen as the neoliberal blueprint for education. Friedman argued that market competition in education would maximise efficiency, responsiveness, and innovation. Friedman saw teachers as producers in a market sense. Colleges sell schooling to students, who are the consumers. Future earnings through increased productivity developed by schooling are a crucial incentive to invest in schooling (Friedman, 1955). Becker (1964, 1993) and human capital theory (Mincer, 1974; Blaug, 1976) of course are very clear that education should be understood as an investment (cost plus effort), which enhances the person's productivity and thus earnings in the labour market. The earnings premium linked to the investment can be calculated with precision and seen as the outcome of market exchanges (education provider-consumer and worker-employer). As Mandler (2020, p. 78) observed, "[T]he most important long-term effect of human capital theory was to draw attention away from education as a consumption good—something people valued because it made for a better life, a more equal society, a fuller sense of citizenship—and fix it in politicians' minds at least as an investment good—something that made the economy grow". This chapter analyses how the concept of neoliberalism has been used to illuminate some of the key changes for HE. It will review some of the most influential accounts of authors who have used the concept of neoliberalism to describe the transformation of HE. Many of these illustrate how public universities have been transformed into neoliberal institutions that have embraced neoliberalism in all their activities. As such, the concept has become pivotal in mounting critiques of the HE system and contemporary universities.

CRITIQUE OF NEOLIBERALISM

Neoliberalism has been applied as a conceptual foundation in a critique of contemporary HE or universities. It becomes part of an argument about what has gone wrong within universities or HE sector as whole and how the sector can fight the perceived growing influence of neoliberalism (see, e.g. Morgan, 2022; Fleming, 2021; Couldry, 2011). An influential text in the United States and a good example of such a critique is Henry Giroux's *Neoliberal War on Higher Education* (2014, see also Giroux, 2007). According to Giroux, neoliberalism is the enemy of HE and has left public institutions in the United States in a terrible state. Giroux argued that neoliberalism has driven the increasing corporatisation of HE and made US universities a market-driven enterprise. The commodification of HE and the drive for profit has eroded the traditional mission of higher education to serve the public good. It has also led to the casualisation of academic labour, with the rise of adjunct and temporary positions and the exploitation of students through high tuition fees and student debt. Additionally, Giroux argued that the emphasis on STEM fields and vocational training has led to a devaluation of the humanities and critical thinking, which are essential for developing informed citizens capable of engaging in democratic society. Giroux's call to arms to fight back against neoliberalism called for a renewed commitment to the public mission of education that emphasises critical thinking, civic engagement, and social justice. He argued elsewhere:

> *Increasingly, neoliberal regimes across Europe and North America have waged a major assault on higher education and those faculty and students who view it as crucial to producing the modes of learning and formative cultures necessary in the struggle for a strong and healthy democracy. For instance, in the United States, higher education is being defunded, devalued and privatized while also restricting access to working- and lower-middle-class students. Those underprivileged students who do have access to some form of post-secondary education are too frequently burdened with financial debts. Increasingly, universities are being turned into accountability factories designed to mimic the values of*

casino capitalism. Disciplines and courses that are not organized around market principles are either being underfunded, cut or refigured to serve market values. (Karlin, 2018)

From this quote, we can see that neoliberalism is in the service of capitalism, and neoliberalism is not just pro-market but also anti-democratic. Although the critique of the role of neoliberalism in HE touches almost all its aspects, I will now outline the five clearest areas where critics of the neoliberal influence on HE have perceived a detrimental effect on HE and HE institutions.

Neoliberalism Transforming Universities

There exists extensive literature either about the nature of so-called 'neoliberal university' (Troiani & Dutson, 2021; Davies et al., 2006; Brooks et al., 2016) or explicitly about how the university has been attacked or shaped by neoliberalism (e.g. Heller, 2016; Giroux, 2014). Within this literature, there is consensus that neoliberalism transformed the university as an organisation irrevocably into a marketised institution that is consumer-driven, with continuous efforts to redesign itself to improve efficiency and accountability as well as international competitiveness (Torres, 2011). Some have placed the workings and aims of universities directly in line with the interest of capitalism (Slaughter & Rhoades, 2004). What they also agree on is that universities are acting more as though they were private corporations, including a greater emphasis on profit making and the commodification of education and research. Walton (2011, p. 24) claimed that "British Universities have become vehicles for further development of corporate capitalism, whose real and present threat to diversity of all kinds extends to universities as well as tropical rainforests, as it prizes measurable growth, a quick fix and the bottom line".

Neoliberal reforms are thought to have diminished the political autonomy of the university, imposing market rationality and consumer choice. Universities had to be reformed to direct their teaching and research according to the dictates of the private sector. Freedom was defined in terms of consumer sovereignty. Universities now struggle to define their objectives outside the realm of the market. More generally, Thrift (2005, p. 23) argued that there are "an increasing number of symmetries between academia and business". The neoliberal university has faced relatively little resistance to welcoming the role of the market sector in (commercial) knowledge production, including private-public partnerships in science production and maximising returns from research.

According to Peters and Jandric (2018, p. 555), the neoliberal university "shifts core commitments of the university from 'the quest for universal truth' and 'the cultural infrastructure for democracy' to 'quality assurance' as defined by the discourse of efficiency and excellence, where neoliberal managerialism becomes the dominant model of knowledge performance". Universities re-orient pedagogical and scholarly activities towards those likely to positively impact these monitoring and measuring performance outcomes and devalue or cover up the social, emotional, and moral impacts without any immediate, measurable performance value. The influence of ranking has frequently been criticised and seen as an instrument of new managerialism or as part of a neoliberal agenda in which market values suppress other aims of education (Gruber, 2014; Vican et al., 2020).

HE as a Private Good

Neoliberalism has supposedly helped end the Keynesian welfare settlement between government, society, and higher education, in which HE was funded and governed as a public good, as it was seen to promote the economic and social welfare of all citizens. Universities used to serve the essential societal function of creating knowledge and promoting social mobility. Attached to this ideal is the idea that universities should remain autonomous institutions with considerable freedom to set their own admission criteria and an overall sense of purpose. As we have seen in Chap. 2, a paramount question within debates about the marketisation of HE is whether higher education is a private or public good (Naidoo & Williams, 2015; Scott, 2016). Collini (2012, p. 198) considered this public good to be a form of value that is something different from economic value, which is involved in "conserving, understanding, extending, and handing on to subsequent generations the intellectual, scientific, and artistic heritage of mankind". Similarly, Peter and Jandric (2018) explained that key aims for the public university between 1960 and 1980 were to construct a knowledgeable citizen and create knowledge that can be used to benefit society. Slaughter and Rhoades (2004, p. 28) likewise observed that HE is shifting from a public good regime characterised by "communalism, universality, the free flow of knowledge and organized skepticism" to an academic capitalist knowledge regime informed by neoliberalism.

Neoliberalism is often interpreted as one that aims to privatise the public sector by moving the public provision of goods and services to the private (Hursh, 2005).

Accepting HE education as a private good is fundamental to neoliberalism. As a private good, it becomes a commodity that ought to be traded in the marketplace, like other commodities. Subsidies and controls of student numbers that distort the market for HE should be eliminated. It then gives impetus to further free up the market for HE, similar to what happened to electricity and gas, telecommunications, and financial services in countries across the globe.

Few would of course deny that education has a public good value and economic meaning that are non-rivalrous and non-excludable—and in education, this means that they are widely accessible and benefitted from. Alternatively, the *private good* refers to the value to the private individual, consumed and utilised for personal use and thus, in most cases, privately funded. From an economic perspective, this reflects an individual's own market preferences and utilities most efficiently organised through competitive markets. Indeed, universities in the Anglo-Saxon context have become increasingly reliant on private funding sources, most notably tuition fees.

In assessing whether HE is a public or private good, we need to know who benefits from it. These discussions are, of course, also relevant to the debate about who funds HE (DBIS, 2009, 2011). HE's benefits for the individual can range from improved health outcomes to future earnings. Society benefits through reduced crime, improved productivity and economic growth, and higher tax income (Willetts, 2017, p. 123).

Marginson (2018) reminds us that there is not much consensus on definitions and conceptions of the public and the private in relation to HE. Those against neoliberalism highlight that many of the benefits are on the level of society and thus not fully private, even if some are economic. They argue that HE should be understood as a public sphere and universities should not be subject to state control and the reach of private interests (Pusser, 2006). Scholars from a range of disciplines have detailed the threat that neoliberalism poses to the fundamental purposes, values, and ideals of education (see, e.g. Boden & Epstein, 2006; Lynch, 2006; Marginson, 1997; Naidoo & Williams, 2015; Natale & Doran, 2012; Potts, 2005). Brown (2011a, p. 123) argued that neoliberalism degrades the concern with the public good: "The more that public universities depend upon corporate funding and formulate their research and educational products as provisioning the market, the less they will serve and promulgate an order of values apart from capital appreciation and profit".

Many scholars highlight the importance of HE in the civic and public spheres, which neoliberalism does not value. In some cases, the death of civil society is ascribed to neoliberalism, and from that perspective, the dismissal of the democratic value of universities (Giroux, 2014). As Lynch (2006, p. 3) argued, neoliberalism "is premised on the assumption that the market can replace the democratic state as the primary producer of cultural logic and value. Neo-liberalism offers a market view of citizenship".

HE institutions have become the victims of a dominating market rationale that discards other aims and purposes, pedagogies, and drives (Edwards & Miller, 1998; Olssen & Peters, 2005). Slaughter and Rhodes (2004) suggested that due to various political, economic, and social policies relating to neoliberalism, HE is shifting from a public good regime characterised by "communalism, universality, the free flow of knowledge, and organized skepticism" (p. 28) to one that commodifies knowledge and aligns more closely with the market.

The Erosion of Academic Work

Another observation linked to neoliberalism is what is perceived as a damaging change in the work conditions academics face in their work (Burton & Bowman, 2022; Davies, 2005; for an earlier account see Parker & Jary, 1995). Modern universities are thought to be constantly measuring and regulating academic performance, which is believed to harm academics' quality of work. Academics are controlled and evaluated in narrow ways driven by perverse performance management, which offers little agency but controls and evaluates at all times (Sousa et al., 2010; Nordbäck et al., 2022). The system is built on competition and competitive ethos with and among individuals, departments, and institutions in HE advanced to uphold accountability in the institution and sector, fragmenting identities in the process (Knights & Clarke, 2014; Kallio et al., 2016). The reduction of academic autonomy is also observed in this context. In the English context, the decline in autonomy can be traced back to the Jarratt Report, which introduced more top-down management and performance metrics. Management practices common in the corporate sector helped erode academics' autonomy and de-professionalised their work (Jarrat, 1985).

Some have gone further and stressed that the corporate model applied to HE institutions will mirror the types of exploitation and extraction with ever greater demands on economic efficiency, and high productivity, aided by anti-unionism (Briziarelli & Flores, 2018, p. 114). Olssen (2000) argued that the contractual professionalism that was the basis for the autonomy and power that academics traditionally enjoyed is at odds with neoliberalism, for neoliberals treat the professions as self-interested groups whose rent-seeking behaviour needs to be curbed. In neoliberalism, power is given through and established by a contract, which is "premised upon a need for compliance, monitoring, and accountability organised in a management line and established through a purchase contract based upon measurable outputs" (Peters, 2017, p. 143). The essence of contractual models involves a specification, which is fundamentally at odds with the notion of professionalism. The regulatory regime no longer values liberal norms and values based on authority and expertise. As we have seen in Chap. 3, the neoliberal distrust of those public-sector workers (although HE is technically not part of the public sector in the UK context) may lead to the erosion of academic labour.

Managerialism

Finally, the use of new managerialist principles that mirror those used in the private sector likewise affects universities. Universities use management principles derived from the private sector to monitor, measure, and evaluate their processes and outputs. Managerialism represents the dominance of the interests of managers within the organisation and the supremacy of management ideas in how they should be run. Managerial principles are not only enacted by managers or management but are also systematically embedded within the organisation as well as its culture. (Shepherd, 2018; Deem, 2001; Deem & Brehony, 2005; Deem et al., 2007). The application of new managerialist principles positions academics as workers rather than as professionals (Olssen et al., 2004). The position of academics has also been increasingly supplanted by administrators (Ginsberg, 2011). As mentioned before, its key features encourage monitoring (including self-monitoring) regimes "through the widespread use of performance indicators" (Barkan, 2018). In Ranson's (2003, p. 468) analysis, the 'era of professionalism' launched 'the age of neoliberalism'. The latter is now driven by a discourse of accountability that supports regimes of audit and measurable outputs (Harvey, 2005; Rhoades & Sporn, 2002) as well as increasingly performance-based management (Lynch, 2014; Dougherty & Natow, 2020). Professional self-regulation has been replaced by hierarchical reporting structures, formalised external audits, and eroding opportunities for professional judgement and autonomy. As explained in Chap. 3, neoliberalism is thought to have shaped the public sector, which is now designed to function as though it were part of the private sector. The new public management (NPM) concept is often used to capture the performance-oriented management approach applied in the UK public sector (and elsewhere) (Gruening, 2001).

Neoliberalism and HE

So far we have seen the use of Neoliberalism to explain and typify the state of HE and has been applied to examine processes ranging from privatisation to the rise of managerialism within HE to increasing consumerism. An alternative approach to clarifying the use of neoliberalism could be based on typology of approaches to Neoliberalism from the previous chapter. Doing so can elucidate the some of the dynamics behind the influence of neoliberalism, as they are understood within each approach.

Neoliberalism a Policy

The first way to understand how neoliberalism has shaped HE is to point at a wider policy doctrine, inserting neoliberal ideas into the policy domain, including governmental organisations and institutions. We can identify areas where policies have shaped the public and education sectors (in some countries, HE is part of the public sector) along neoliberal lines. For scholars in the field of education, neoliberalism is a policy rationale of an active erosion of a range of institutions and practices deemed 'public' in the previously liberal welfare state settlements (Gerrard, 2015). Many have observed the dismantling of public schools, the injection of 'choice' to support competition, and high-stakes accountability aimed at driving families away from public education (Baltodano, 2014; Hursh & Henderson, 2011; Lipman, 2007).

The neoliberal call for greater use of the market as an efficient solution to social and economic problems has shaped the educational sector (Gewirtz et al., 1995; Hursh, 2005; Robertson, 2000). Neoliberalism seeks to make existing markets wider and to create new markets where they did not exist before (Connell, 2013). Neoliberal policy aims to bring institutions and activities outside of the market inside the market. Education is only one of them. There is a need to reinvent education in a 'market-like' way where educational institutions cannot be privatised. Olssen (2001) outlined how neoliberalism has shaped education policy practice in New Zealand through the power of its central state authority. Klees (2008) provided an overview of US educational policies that the author identifies with neoliberalism, including knowledge management, merit pay, reformation of civil service laws, community involvement, decentralisation, increased testing, vouchers, and privatisation. Peck (2015, p. 589) observed that in the United States, Reagan's administration promoted neoliberal educational reform through market-driven strategies of deregulation, privatisation, high-stakes test-based evaluations, and weakened teacher tenure and seniority rights. Ball (2017, p. 86) saw a 'neoliberal outlook' within British education policy as antagonistic force against the welfare state and for the promotion of market-led economic growth. Markets and private interests are brought in partnership with the state in the provision of education.

Markets and choice have been used by policymakers as a panacea to make schools more efficient and improve performance. Whitty et al. (1998) (as cited in Hursh, 2005, p. 4) wrote that "within the range of political rationales, it is the neoliberal alternative which dominates, as does a particular emphasis on market mechanisms". In this line of thinking, policymakers become active agents in dictating how universities operate. Political ideas about the supposed wastefulness of public institutions and the virtues of letting market incentives improve how institutions perform and improve citizens' self-reliance have led to the restructuring of public-sector institutions. Therefore, it is easy to see how these same political pressures were brought to bear on universities to fall in line with the market and emulate practices from the corporate sector. We saw in Chap. 2 that from Thatcher onwards, English universities had to be reformed to direct their teaching and research according to the dictates of the private sector and impose market rationality and consumer choice, which we will further explore in the next chapter.

Neoliberalism as Ideology

For the second approach, neoliberalism as ideology, changes in HE are driven by a wider ideological battle to change people's thinking about the role of the state and markets in their lives. Broader ideal forces within society and the economy adhere to the principles of neoliberalism (Saunders, 2010) and have changed how people understand the aims of HE.[1] The pervasiveness of economic rationality culminates in the "saturat[ion] of our consciousness, so that the educational, economic, and social world we see and interact with, and the commonsense interpretations we put on it, becomes [...] the only world" (Apple, 2004, p. 4). Many changes were supported by, and congruent with, a neoliberal ideology that has permeated society. The neoliberal worldview affects and penetrates all areas where markets were previously deemed inappropriate or illogical. Neoliberalism, as a capitalist ideology, must first change the idea that education is a public good. Instead, it needs to be seen as a market commodity in which consumers actively choose the product according to their market preferences. We can see a wide range of authors using neoliberalism in this manner. Political theorist Wendy Brown (2011) highlighted that the neoliberal rationale has affected the whole public domain, including the public sector, education, and democratic institutions. She stated:

> *[M]ore than economic policy, neoliberalism is a governing social and political rationality that submits all human activities, values, institutions, and practices to market principles. It formulates everything in terms of capital investment and appreciation (including, and especially, humans themselves) [...] As a governing rationality, neoliberalism extends from the management of the state itself to the soul of the subject; it renders health, education, transportation, nature, and art into individual consumer goods, and converts patients, students, drivers, athletes, and museum-goers alike into entrepreneurs of their own needs and desires who consumer or invest in these goods.* (Brown, 2011b, p. 118)

Likewise, Fabricant and Brier (2016, p. 91) declared that "neoliberal ideology has seeped into the governance and practices of most public agencies, where it has borrowed strategies from the business sector that focus on efficiency, increased productivity, and metrics of accountability and measurable outcomes". According to the authors, this has affected how US universities operate with a lack of investment in public universities and the growth in tuition fees which affects students from disadvantaged backgrounds, warning that "the conjunction of fiscal austerity, imposition of a neoliberal business model, and consequent institutional restructuring has resulted in public higher education becoming an active agent in the growth rather than reduction of social inequality" (Fabricant & Bier, 2016, p. 118).

The neoliberal university (or corporate university, e.g. Aronowitz, 2001) has remained a popular concept (e.g. Slaughter & Rhoades, 2000; Fleming, 2021; Kezar et al., 2019). Proponents argue that educational institutions have been entirely taken over by neoliberalism. Universities behave like corporations, cannibalising the academic culture traditionally based on collegiality and collaboration, now dominated by managerialism. The neoliberal university defines itself within market parameters (including income, efficiency, and profitability) and is no longer involved in civic engagement.

Neoliberalism as Governmentality

As we have seen, the notion of governmentality has been influential, particularly in explaining how neoliberalism can permeate society. Many have used the concept of governmentality in the context of universities and the production of academic and student subjectivities (e.g. Davies, 2005; Archer, 2008; Davies & Bansel, 2010; Ball, 2012; Morrissey, 2013; Krause-Jenson & Garsten, 2014; Cannizzo, 2015; Knights & Clarkes, 2014). Studies specifically on the marketisation of HE frequently utilise the concept of governmentality to critically evaluate its consequences (e.g. Bragg, 2007; Yokoyama, 2008). As governmentality, neoliberalism can be understood in terms of political rationalities mediated through discourses acted upon through a range of political technologies—the strategies, techniques, and procedures by which political programmes are put in place. Under neoliberalism, governments take less responsibility for the welfare of the individual. The individual becomes responsible for themselves, an active entrepreneur of the self who capitalises on their existence through calculated acts and investments (Rose, 1999).

Neoliberalism as a form of governmentality has been applied to HE, often drawing parallels as it operates in the public sector (Olssen et al., 2004; Varman et al., 2011; Wilkins, 2012). Many have made us Foucauldian conceptual approach to understanding how neoliberal governmentality is shaping HE (Peters, 2001, 2003; Morrisey, 2013). Some have looked at some of the language used within HE to demarcate a shift in how individuals experience education. Gray et al. (2018) observed that the language of neoliberalism has penetrated education as we know it and that market concepts such as *quality control, impact, knowledge transfer, human capital, deregulation, entrepreneur, choice, customer,* and *stakeholder* have replaced other terms and taken over education. The concept of choice, especially, is ubiquitous. Ball (2012, p. 18) stated, "neoliberalism gets into our minds and our souls, into the ways in which we think about what we do, and into our social relations with others. It is about how we relate to our students and our colleagues and our participation in new courses and forms of pedagogy and our 'knowledge production'".

For Foucault, neoliberalism relies on understanding the world in which enterprising subjects *invest* in their human capital, mainly through education. Ball (2017, p. 217) drew on this idea when he noted that the neoliberal regime of governmentality in education has resulted in "an investment model that requires students, teachers, and schools to make decisions about how they invest their time, resources, and energy in relation to likely returns—as qualifications and labour market opportunities, as performance improvement, as social advantage. Individuals and families must take responsibility for their own performance and their own improvement".

Akin to how neoliberalism has shaped the modern citizen (Ong, 2006; Mavelli, 2022), the neoliberal university shapes one of its users in particular: the students. Neoliberal universities create their own neoliberal subjects. The neoliberal student is shaped as a subject by neoliberalism. Often, students are portrayed as a neoliberal *Homo oeconomicus* who *"is an entrepreneur, an entrepreneur of himself, being for himself his own capital, being for himself his own producer, being for himself the source of [his] earnings"* (Foucault, 2008, pp. 225–226). The way HE is discussed throughout society produces a student subject, primarily a market actor who places 'choice' and the 'entrepreneurial self' in their learner identities. As such, the neoliberal student is compelled to deal with and adapt to constantly changing education and workplaces (Nairn & Higgins, 2007, p. 264). The understanding of HE participation as *investment* has strengthened within society in general, and in policy circles specifically (Tholen, 2022). Within neoliberalism as a governmentality approach, students are thought to take on the neoliberal repertoires of the self and are driven by being enterprising and competitive. Instead of developing an ethical and well-rounded individual, as put forward by the *Bildung tradition,* the student understands themselves primarily as a market actor, encouraged to economically capitalise the self (Peters, 2005). Students become self-reliant and entrepreneurial actors investing in HE to improve their prospects in the market (Heller, 2016), marking the individualisation of responsibility for labour market outcomes (Spohrer, 2011). Others position the student as a customer of HE, again altering how all actors within education understand themselves, the education on offer, and HE institutions (e.g. van Andel et al., 2012).

Conclusion

Despite the common usage of the term 'neoliberalism' within the literature on HE, it often remains rather undefined, serving as a synonym for marketisation, commercialisation, or privatisation. As part of a critique, neoliberalism has been portrayed as the prime cause of harmful or corrosive elements within HE reform. Alternatively, it has been used to signify a general economic instrumentality rather than to make explici the role of markets and competition as expressions of freedom and responsibility. It is important to note that not all critics of the erosion of academic work and the market-driven approach to governance use the concept of neoliberalism to understand these developments. For those who do, many do not aim to elucidate the mechanism behind the neoliberal power force that transformed the sector. Too often, the commodified neoliberal university is presented as an endgame in which universities are now entirely controlled by neoliberalism and fixated exclusively on neoliberal aims and values. This seems implausible. If we want to understand the role of neoliberalism in marketisation specifically, we need to be very explicit and recognise the complicated nature of the concept. There is a need to assess how the marketisation of HE relates to forces we can identify as neoliberal, to which we turn in the next chapter.

Note

1. Of course, the state has a role to play in how capitalism develops and also influences how capitalism shapes HE sectors (Schulze-Cleven et al., 2017).

References

van Andel, J., Pimentel Botas, C., Huisman, J., & J. (2012). The consumption values of and empowerment of student as customer in higher education: Taking a rational look inside 'Pandora's Box'. *Higher Education Review, 45*(1), 62–85.

Apple, M. (2004). *Ideology and Curriculum*. Routledge Falmer.

Aranowitz, S. (2001). *The Knowledge Factory: Dismantling the Corporate University and Creating True Higher Learning*. Beacon Press.

Archer, L. (2008). The new neoliberal subjects? Young/er academics' constructions of professional identity. *Journal of Education Policy, 23*(3), 265–285.

Ball, S. J. (2012). Performativity, commodification, and commitment: An I-Spy guide to the neoliberal university. *British Journal of Educational Studies, 60*(1), 17–28.

Ball, S. J. (2017). *The Education Debate – Policy and Politics in the Twenty-First Century* (3rd ed.). Bristol University Press.

Baltodano, M. P. (2014). Neoliberalism and the demise of public education: The corporatization of schools of education. In D. Blum & C. Ullman (Eds.), *The globalization and corporatization of education: Limits and Liminality of the Market Mantra* (pp. 121–141). Routledge.

Barkan, J. (2018). Corporate power and neoliberalism. In D. Cahill, M. Cooper, M. Konings, & D. Primrose (Eds.), *The Sage handbook of neoliberalism* (pp. 446–456). Sage.

Becker, G. S. (1964). *Human capital: A Theoretical and Empirical Analysis, with Special Reference to Education*. Chicago University Press.

Becker, G. S. (1993). The economic way of looking at behavior. *Journal of Political Economy, 101*(3), 385–409.

Blaug, M. (1976). The empirical status of human capital theory: A slightly jaundiced survey. *Journal of Economic Literature, 14*(3), 827–855.

Boden, R., & Epstein, D. (2006). Managing the research imagination? Globalisation and research in higher education. *Globalisation, Societies and Education, 4*(2), 223–236.

Bragg, S. (2007). Student voice and governmentality: The production of enterprising subject. *Discourse: Studies in the Cultural Politics of Education, 28*(3), 343–355.

Briziarelli, M., & Flores, J. L. (2018). Professing contradictions: Knowledge work and the-neoliberal condition of academic workers. *TripleC Communication, Capitalism and Critique, 16*(1), 114–128.

Brooks, R., Byford, K., & Sela, K. (2016). Students' unions, consumerism and the neo-liberal university. *British Journal of Sociology of Education, 37*(8), 1211–1228.

Brown, R. (Ed.). (2011a). *Higher Education and the Market*. Routledge.

Brown, W. (2011b). Neoliberalized knowledge. *History of the Present, 1*(1), 113–129.

Burton, S., & Bowman, B. (2022). The academic precariat: Understanding life and labour in the neoliberal academy. *British Journal of Sociology of Education, 43*(4), 497–512.

Cannizzo, F. (2015). Academic subjectivities: Governmentality and self-development in higher education. *Foucault Studies, 20*, 199–217.

Collini, S. (2012). *What Are Universities For?* Penguin.

Connell, R. (2013). The neoliberal cascade and education: An essay on the market agenda and its consequences. *Critical Studies in Education, 54*(2), 99–112.

Couldry, N. (2011). Fighting for the university's life. In M. Bailey & D. Freedman (Eds.), *The Assault on Universities: A Manifesto for Resistance* (pp. 37–48). Pluto.

Davies, B. (2005). The (im)possibility of intellectual work in neoliberal regimes. *Discourse: Studies in the Cultural Politics of Education, 26*(1), 1–14.

Davies, B., & Bansel, P. (2007). Neoliberalism and education. *International Journal of Qualitative Studies in Education, 20*(3), 247–259.
Davies, B., & Bansel, P. (2010). Governmentality and academic work: Shaping the hearts and minds of academic workers. *Journal of Curriculum Theorizing, 26*(3), 5–20.
Davies, B., Gottsche, M., & Bansel, P. (2006). The Rise and Fall of the Neo-Liberal University. *European Journal of Education, 41*(2), 305–319.
Deem, R. (2001). 'Globalisation, new managerialism, academic capitalism and entrepreneurialism in universities: Is the local dimension still important? *Comparative Education, 37*(1), 7–20.
Deem, R., & Brehony, K. J. (2005). Management as ideology: The case of "new managerialism" in higher education. *Oxford Review of Education, 31*(2), 217–235.
Deem, R., Hillyard, S., & Reed, M. I. (2007). *Knowledge, Higher Education, and the New Managerialism: The Changing Management of UK Universities.* Oxford University Press.
Department for Business, Innovation and Skills (DBIS). (2009). *Higher Ambitions: The Future of Universities in a Knowledge Economy.* DBIS.
Department for Business, Innovation and Skills (DBIS). (2011). *Students at the Heart of the System.* DBIS.
Dougherty, K. J., & Natow, R. S. (2020). Performance-based funding for higher education: How well does neoliberal theory capture neoliberal practice? *Higher Education, 80*(3), 457–478.
Edwards, T. J., & Miller, H. (1998). Change in mass higher education: University, state and economy. In D. Jary & M. Parker (Eds.), *The New Higher Education: Issues and Directions for the Post- Dearing University* (pp. 41–62). Staffordshire University Press.
Fabricant, M., & Brier, S. (2016). *Austerity Blues: Fighting for the Soul of Public Higher Education.* Johns Hopkins University Press.
Fleming, P. (2021). The ghost university: Academe from the ruins. *Emancipations: A Journal of Critical Social Analysis, 1*(1) article 4.
Foucault, M. (2008). *The Birth of Biopolitics: Lectures at the Collège de France, 1978–79.* Palgrave.
Friedman, M. (1955). The role of government in education. In R. A. Solo (Ed.), *Economics and the Public Interest* (pp. 85–107). Rutgers University Press.
Gerrard, J. (2015). Public education in neoliberal times: Memory and desire. *Journal of Education Policy, 30*(6), 855–868.
Gewirtz, S., Ball, S. J., & Bowe, R. (1995). *Markets, Choice, and Equity in Education.* Open University Press.
Ginsberg, B. (2011). *The Fall of the Faculty: The Rise of the All-Administrative University and Why it Matters.* Oxford University Press.
Giroux, H. A. (2007). *The University in Chains: Confronting the Military-Industrial-Academic Complex.* Paradigm.

Giroux, H. A. (2014). *Neoliberalism's War on Higher Education*. Haymarket Books.
Gray, J., O'Regan, J. P., & Wallace, C. (2018). Education and the discourse of global neoliberalism. *Language and Intercultural Communication, 18*(5), 471–477.
Gruber, T. (2014). Academic sell-out: How an obsession with metrics and rankings is damaging academia. *Journal of Marketing for Higher Education, 24*(2), 165–177.
Gruening, G. (2001). Origin and theoretical basis of new public management. *International Public Management Journal, 4*(1), 1–25.
Harvey, D. A. (2005). *A Brief History of Neoliberalism*. Oxford University Press.
Hayek, F. (2006). *The Constitution of Liberty*. Routledge.
Heller, H. (2016). *The Capitalist University: The Transformations of Higher Education in the United States since 1945*. Pluto.
Hill, D. (2003). Global neo-liberalism, the deformation of education and resistance. *The Journal of Critical Education Policy Studies, 1*(1), 1–28.
Hursh, D. (2005). Neo-liberalism, markets and accountability: Transforming education and undermining democracy in the United States and England. *Policy Futures in Education, 3*(1), 3–15.
Hursh, D. W., & Henderson, J. A. (2011). Contesting global neoliberalism and creating alternative futures. *Discourse: Studies in the Cultural Politics of Education, 32*(2), 171–185.
Jarrat, A. (1985). *Report of the Steering Committee for Efficiency Studies in Universities*. HMSO.
Kallio, K.-M., Kallio, T. J., Tienari, J., & Hyvönen, T. (2016). Ethos at stake: Performance management and academic work in universities. *Human Relations, 69*(3), 685–709.
Karlin, M. (2018). Henry A. Giroux: The nightmare of neoliberal fascism. *Truthout*, June 10. Retrieved April 22, 2024, from https://truthout.org/articles/henry-a-giroux-the-nightmare-of-neoliberal-fascism/
Kezar, A. (2004). Obtaining integrity? Reviewing and examining the charter between higher education and society. *The Review of Higher Education, 27*(4), 429–459.
Kezar, A., Scott, D., & DePaola, T. (2019). *The Gig Academy: Mapping Labor in the Neoliberal University*. John Hopkins University Press.
Klees, S. J. (2008). A quarter century of neoliberal thinking in education: Misleading analyses and failed policies. *Globalisation, Societies, and Education, 6*(4), 311–348.
Knights, D., & Clarke, C. A. (2014). It's a bittersweet symphony, this life: Fragile academic selves and insecure identities at work. *Organization Studies, 35*(3), 335–357.
Krause-Jenson, J., & Garsten, C. (2014). Introduction: Neoliberal turns in higher education. *Learning and Teaching, 7*(3), 1–13.

Levidow, L. (2005). Neoliberal agendas for higher education. In A. Saad-Filho & D. Johnston (Eds.), *Neoliberalism: A Critical Reader* (pp. 156–163). Pluto Press.

Lipman, P. (2007). "No child left behind": Globalization, privatization, and the politics of inequality. In E. W. Ross & R. Gibson (Eds.), *Neoliberalism and Education Reform* (pp. 35–58). Hampton Press.

Lynch, K. (2006). Neo-liberalism and marketisation: The implications for higher education. *European Educational Research Journal, 5*(1), 1–17.

Lynch, K. (2014). "New managerialism" in education: The organisational form of neoliberalism'. *Open Democracy*, September 16. Retrieved April 24, 2024, from https://www.opendemocracy.net/kathleen-lynch/'new-managerialism'-in-education-organisational-form-of-neoliberalism

Mandler, P. (2020). *The Crisis of the Meritocracy. Britain's Transition to Mass Education Since the Second World War*. Oxford University Press. 2020.

Marginson, S. (1997). *Markets in Education*. Allen and Unwin.

Marginson, S. (2018). Public/private in higher education: A synthesis of economic and political approaches. *Studies in Higher Education, 43*(2), 322–337.

Mavelli, L. (2022). *Neoliberal Citizenship: Sacred Markets, Sacrificial Lives*. Oxford University Press.

McLaren, P. (2005). *Capitalist and Conquerors: A Critical Pedagogy Against Empire*. Rowman and Littlefield.

Mincer, J. (1974). *Schooling, Experience, and Earnings*. Columbia University Press.

Morgan, H. (2022). Neoliberalism's influence on American universities: How the business model harms students and society. *Policy Futures in Education, 20*(2), 149–165.

Morrissey, J. (2013). Governing the academic subject: Foucault, governmentality and the performing university. *Oxford Review of Education, 39*(6), 797–810.

Naidoo, R., & Williams, J. (2015). The neoliberal regime in English higher education: Charters, consumers and the erosion of the public good. *Critical Studies in Education, 56*(2), 208–223.

Nairn, K., & Higgins, J. (2007). New Zealand's neoliberal generation: Tracing discourses of economic (ir)rationality. *International Journal of Qualitative Studies in Education, 20*(3), 261–281.

Natale, S. M., & Doran, C. (2012). Marketisation of education: An ethical dilemma. *Journal of Business Ethics, 105*(2), 187–196.

Nordbäck, E., Hakonen, M., & Tienari, J. (2022). Academic identities and sense of place: A collaborative autoethnography in the neoliberal university. *Management Learning, 53*(2), 331–349.

Olssen, M. (2000). The neo-liberal appropriation of tertiary education policy: Accountability, research and academic freedom. *Access: Contemporary Issues in Education, 19*(2), 142–188.

Olssen, M. (2001). *The Neo-liberal Appropriation of Tertiary Education Policy: Accountability, Research and Academic Freedom. State-of-the-Art Monograph, no. 8, October.* New Zealand Association for Research in Education.

Olssen, M., Codd, J., & O'Neill, A.-M. (2004). *Education Policy: Globalization, Citizenship and Democracy.* Sage.

Olssen, M., Peters, M. A., & M.A. (2005). Neoliberalism, higher education and the knowledge economy: from the free market to knowledge capitalism. *Journal of Education Policy, 20*(3), 313–345.

Ong, A. (2006). *Neoliberalism as Exception: Mutations in Citizenship and Sovereignty.* Duke University Press.

Parker, M., & Jary, D. (1995). The McUniversity: Organisations, management and academic subjectivity. *Organization, 2*(2), 319–338.

Peck, J. (2015). (Neo) liberalism, popular media, and the political struggle for the future of US-public education. *European Journal of Communication, 30*(5), 587–603.

Peters, M. A. (2001). Foucault and governmentality: Understanding the neoliberal paradigm of education policy. *The School Field, 12*(5/6), 61–72.

Peters, M. A. (2003). Truth-telling as an educational practice of the self: Foucault, parrhesia and the ethics of subjectivity. *Oxford Review of Education, 29*(2), 207–223.

Peters, M. A. (2005). The new prudentialism in education: Actuarial rationality and the entrepreneurial self. *Educational Theory, 55*(2), 123–137.

Peters, M. A. (2017). From state responsibility for education and welfare to self-responsibilisation in the market. *Discourse: Studies in the Cultural Politics of Education, 38*(1), 138–145.

Peters, M. A., & Jandric, P. (2018). Neoliberalism and the university. In D. Cahill, M. Cooper, M. Konings, & D. Primrose (Eds.), *The Sage Handbook of Neoliberalism* (pp. 553–564). Sage.

Potts, M. (2005). The consumerist subversion of education. *Academic Questions, 18*(3), 54–64.

Pusser, B. (2006). Reconsidering higher education and the public good: The role of public spheres. In W. G. Tierney (Ed.), *Governance and the Public Good* (pp. 11–28). State University of New York Press.

Ranson, S. (2003). Public accountability in the age of neo-liberal governance. *Journal of Education Policy, 18*(5), 459–480.

Rhoades, R., Sporn, B., & B. (2002). Quality assurance in Europe and the US: Professional and political economic framing of higher education policy. *Higher Education, 43*(3), 355–390.

Robertson, S. (2000). *A Class Act Changing Teachers Work, the State, and Globalisation.* Falmer.

Rose, N. (1999). *Powers of Freedom: Reframing Political Thought.* Cambridge University Press.

Saunders, D. B. (2010). Neoliberal ideology and public higher education in the United States. *Journal for Critical Education Policy Studies, 8*(1), 41–77.
Schulze-Cleven, T., Reitz, T., & Maesse, J. et al. (2017). The new political economy of higher education: between distributional conflicts and discursive stratification. *Higher Education 73*, 795–812.
Scott, P. (2016). Private commodities and public goods: Markets and values in higher education. In P. Johnand & J. Fanghanel (Eds.), *Dimensions of Marketisation in Higher Education* (pp. 15–25). Routledge.
Shepherd, S. (2018). Managerialism: An ideal type. *Studies in Higher Education, 43*(9), 1668–1678.
Slaughter, S., & Rhoades, G. (2000). The Neo-liberal University. *New Labor Forum, 6*(Spring–Summer), 73–79.
Slaughter, S., & Rhoades, G. (2004). *Academic Capitalism and the New Economy: Markets, State and Higher Education*. Johns Hopkins University Press.
Sousa, C. A., de Nijs, W. F., & Hendriks, P. H. (2010). Secrets of the beehive: Performance management in university research organizations. *Human Relations, 63*(9), 1439–1460.
Spohrer, K. (2011). Deconstructing 'Aspiration': UK policy debates and european policy trends. *European Educational Research Journal, 10*(1), 53–63.
Tholen, G. (2022). *Modern Work and the Marketisation of Higher Education*. Policy Press.
Thrift, N. (2005). *Knowing Capitalism*. Sage.
Torres, C. A. (2011). Public universities and the neoliberal common sense: Seven iconoclastic theses. *International Studies in Sociology of Education, 21*(3), 177–197.
Troiani, I., & Dutson, C. (2021). The neoliberal university as a space to learn/think/work in higher education. *Architecture and Culture, 9*(1), 5–23.
Varman, R., Saha, B., & Skålén, P. (2011). Market subjectivity and neoliberal governmentality in higher education. *Journal of Marketing Management, 27*(11–12), 1163–1185.
Vican, S., Friedman, A., & Andreasen, R. (2020). Metrics, money, and managerialism: Faculty experiences of competing logics in higher education. *The Journal of Higher Education, 91*(1), 139–164.
Walton, J. K. (2011). The idea of the university. In M. Bailey & D. Freedman (Eds.), *The Assault on Universities* (pp. 15–26). Pluto.
Wilkins, A. (2012). The spectre of neoliberalism: Pedagogy, gender and the construction of learner identities. *Critical Studies in Education, 53*(2), 197–210.
Willetts, D. (2017). *A University Education*. Oxford University Press.
Yokoyama, K. (2008). Neo-liberal governmentality in the English and Japanese higher education. *International Studies in Sociology of Education, 18*(3), 231–247.

CHAPTER 5

How Can We Understand the Role of Neoliberalism in the Marketisation of HE?

Abstract This chapter is dedicated to the concept of marketisation in HE and its relation to neoliberalism. Drawing on the previous chapter, it offers an assessment of the idea that neoliberalism is the driver of marketisation. The chapter differentiates five areas: market, competition, finance, the state, and universities. Each will show that different approaches to neoliberalism fit these themes best.

Keywords Marketisation • Higher Education • Marketisation • Markets • Competition

In the previous chapter, we saw how and why the concept of neoliberalism has been so influential in understanding HE: despite the looseness of the concept when applied to the HE sector, it has offered many social scientists an analytical framework to come to grips with a wide-ranging set of changes in education.

This chapter examines the concept of marketisation, which is often perceived as a (pure) consequence of neoliberalism. Others see it even as *part of* neoliberalism, in other words, as a process within the wider neoliberal project. Given the centrality of the free market in neoliberalism, it is quite logical to think that marketisation is a typical neoliberal phenomenon.

© The Author(s), under exclusive license to Springer Nature Switzerland AG 2024
G. Tholen, *The Role of Neoliberalism in the Marketisation of Higher Education*, Palgrave Studies on Global Policy and Critical Futures in Education, https://doi.org/10.1007/978-3-031-66281-2_5

Neoliberalism is defined as the promotion of markets; any marketisation seems neoliberal by definition. Indeed, there are many examples in the literature where marketisation is assumed, without much justification, to be a neoliberal phenomenon. This raises two issues. First, as we saw in Chap. 3, the role of the market in neoliberalism is specific and distinct from pro-market approaches such as classical liberalism of free marketeer positions. Second, how markets are used in neoliberalist theory may differ from how they are used and understood by students, governments, universities, etc. Competition has always been part of scientific research and university education long before the so-called neoliberal turn. How, why, and to what extent are markets and forms of competition introduced and sustained? How and to what extent can neoliberalism be reasonably understood as part of neoliberalism or as an outcome of neoliberalism?

The concern about the development, expansion, and extension of markets is what drives many neoliberal ideas, so how it can do so matters. Biebrichter (2018, p. 26) stated that all accounts of neoliberalism share the problem of identifying the factors indispensable to the maintenance of functioning markets, given that they cannot be left to their own devices. In the previous chapter, we saw that the intervention of the state is essential, as is the role of the individual in their entrepreneurial capacity. Again, using the three different approaches to neoliberalism can offer insight into how marketisation can be understood through a neoliberal lens.

Marketisation

Marketisation in HE has happened over several decades (Tholen, 2022). It has been widely acknowledged as a key phenomenon in modern HE systems (Brown, 2011a; Lynch, 2006; McGettigan, 2013; Molesworth et al., 2010). Two key areas of marketisation: the rise of user-pay finance and increasing commodification. Shifting the costs of HE education to the users, namely, the students, shapes whether the market should coordinate education provision. Once the cost of HE has been transferred to its users rather than from public funds, it positions the institution and students differently in relation to each other. The market-consumer relationship provides a blueprint for how each of them should behave.

The idea that university education must be treated as a product akin to other products in the service sector and traded in a marketplace for HE is increasingly accepted and integrated into how the university functions (Henkel, 1997; Bok, 2003; Dill, 2003; Komljenovic, 2020). As Lynch

(2006, p. 2) explained, "Commercialisation is normalised and its operational values and purposes have been encoded in the systems of all types of universities". Degrees are increasingly seen as products to be sold to consumers (i.e. students) by providers (universities) (Naidoo & Jamieson, 2005). Students are expected to behave like rational market actors, which drives the need for further transparency and detailed market information so that students can make sound and well-informed decisions in the marketplace.

The Role of Markets

Marketisation is built on the assumption that markets 'know best' where the resources need to be allocated. Paying students are thought to be financially motivated actors incentivised to optimise decisions on their HE investments. Markets are deemed to stimulate raising standards, delivery, and achievement (Dill, 1997; Williams, 1997). HE must respond to students' needs and preferences or lose business. HE institutions must continuously seek to gain an advantage in the market in terms of quality of service (or, in theory, price). As a result, they become more attentive to students.

Market reforms in the English higher education system came into force through government policies in which HE institutions were able to differentiate themselves through tuition fees. The HE Act 2004 (HM Government, 2004) led to the replacement of a fixed rate of £1125 with variable fees between 0 and £3000. This was followed by the 2011 White Paper titled 'Students at the Heart of the System' (DBIS, 2011) permitting HE institutions in England to triple their annual tuition fees from £3000 to £9000. With the reduction in teaching grants, the government's control over student numbers was loosened. Universities could enrol unlimited numbers of students who achieved at least AAB A-level grades or equivalent (extended to ABB the following year), expecting that only a small group of 'elite' institutions would charge the maximum of £9,000. Instead, all the institutions charged this.

Later White Papers (DBIS, 2016) created additional incentives to differentiate the market and remove the barriers for "challenger" providers to enter the HE market. The 2016 White Paper titled 'Success as a Knowledge Economy' introduced policies centred on improving the accessibility and quality of HE through market and choice. For instance, it proposed to make it easier to set up 'high-quality' universities, which would give students more choice. The paper directly argued for greater competition between providers, improving efficiency and teaching quality within the marketplace, and offering students more choices in the type of education they want. The HE and Research Act 2017 that followed reiterated that competition is the best option to improve quality, participation, and responsiveness. A key aim was to establish a regulatory 'architecture' for an HE market built on competition and choice, replacing existing HE regulatory systems with a new single regulator. The Office for Students (OfS) was created to regulate the new student market, oversee whether competition and choice were expressed in the system, and assess quality and standards.

Recent policy changes were actively intended to "create an open, market-based and affordable system, with more competition and innovation, and a level playing field for new providers" (DBIS, 2015, p. 57). It identified a need to construct a market in which universities offered courses in which their consumers would choose programmes with high standards. Providers who did not offer good value would lose customers and, therefore, revenue. There have been continuous efforts to even close the competitive market to those providing low-quality courses (DfE, 2023a). The assumption here is that the least popular are of the lowest quality.

The private higher education sector has also seen the growth of private providers in the HE landscape (Hunt & Boliver, 2023). The White Paper 'Success as a Knowledge Economy' (DBIS, 2016) set out how private providers would be able to compete with public HE providers on a level playing field. This materialised in the 2017 Higher Education and Research Act. Again, the key rationale for allowing more private providers to offer HE courses was to develop a market in which new high-quality challenger institutions could enter the market and award their own degrees (DBIS, 2016, p. 6). However, currently, the share of students in HE enrolled with them remains small (Bolton, 2024, p. 32).

Real Free Market?

In theory, the price mechanism within a free market serves as an indicator of under- and over-supply as well as an incentive for producers to produce goods for which there is an established demand. Markets are a fast and efficient method of supplying information on consumer demand to which producers and providers respond (Hayek, 1945). For some neoliberals, such as Friedman, the idea of free and pure markets is more of a utopian quality that helps us move towards freer markets (and societies). Yet many have pointed out that there is no perfect free market in HE and that fundamental obstacles are often to be found in the nature of education itself (Agasisti & Catalano, 2006; Brown, 2013; Marginson, 2013; McGettigan, 2013; Molesworth et al., 2010). Brown (2011b, p. 22) identified various limitations on the application of the theory of markets to HE, such as the mix of public and individual advantages, the need for regulation on market entry and competition, and the lack of valid and reliable information about quality.

There are some crucial differences from real free markets. The English HE system as a market for education does not work fully or perfectly (Marginson, 2013; Brown, 2013; McGettigan, 2013).[1] HE institutions have remained charitable organisations, as Williams (2013, p. 6) pointed out. According to Jongbloed (2003), there are eight conditions for a market, and all of these conditions tend to facilitate competition between institutions, which boils down to the freedom of both HE institutions and students to make decisions. From a provider's point of view, they should have freedom of entry into the marketplace, specify the product, use resources, and determine prices. From a consumer's point of view, customers should be free to choose a provider and a product, have adequate information about the costs and the quality, be able to pay directly, and prices should cover costs (Jongbloed, 2003). Brown and Scott (2009, p. 3) stated that a full market in HE would have the following:

A. Little or no regulation of market entry (so plenty of market competition, including from profit and 'for-profit' providers);
B. No regulatory limits on the prices charged (fees) or the numbers enrolled;
C. The cost of teaching would be met entirely through fees which approximate to average costs (rather than through a combination of fees and grants to institutions);
D. The cost of fees would be met from users' (students and/or their sponsors) own resources: there would be no subsidies from the taxpayer;
E. Users would decide what, where, and how to study on the basis of effective (valid, reliable, and accessible) information about the price, quality, and availability of relevant programmes and providers.

Regarding (A), currently, there is high regulation of market entry in the English context. For instance, there remain entrance requirements, so unlike a free market, there are barriers (in the form of entry requirements, in most cases driven by A-level/BTEC grades). As for (B), there is a distinct regulatory limit on the fees but not the student numbers in most undergraduate courses. The removal of the cap on student numbers is built on the idea that participation in HE is inherently positive for both individuals and society: "By lifting the cap on student numbers we have ensured that England's world-class higher education system is open to anyone with the potential to benefit from it" (DBIS, 2015, p. 35).

The cost of teaching (C) is largely met entirely through fees, although there have been complaints that the level of undergraduate tuition fees no longer covers the costs of providing undergraduate programmes (Fazackerley, 2023). The fees have been frozen since 2017, and despite urgent warnings from universities, the government is unlikely to increase the cap on fees (Weale, 2023). The cost of fees is largely met by the users, with minimal subsidies from the taxpayer (D). The teaching costs of HE are therefore largely privatised. However, there is still uncertainty regarding the extent to which graduates will actually repay their loans (Morgan, 2022). Finally, it is unclear what counts as effective (valid, reliable, and accessible) information about the price, quality, and availability of relevant programmes and providers (E). It is undoubtedly challenging to produce valid and reliable information about the quality of different subjects, institutions, and programmes. Education is often seen as what economists call a (post) experience good, in which buyers can only assess the quality after purchase and/or after it is consumed. It is very difficult to make valid comparisons regarding quality and learning achievement between different disciplines and institutions. Finding reliable data (which are often created by institutions themselves) is also not straightforward. However, there are many other markets where consumers have information that is far from perfect (information asymmetry). The used car market is a classic example, but the healthcare market could be another.

Despite the freedom of providers to set prices for their services, there is currently no competition on price. Price system markets are constituted by laws of supply and demand. Unlike a free market, the supply side (i.e. consumers) does have a choice, but it is limited to the offer available to them. As Bowl (2018, p. 5) pointed out, "the idea of a pure market in HE, as in other areas of what was once regarded as public-sector provision, is more imaginary than real". According to the author, although business principles increasingly drive universities, they are not dedicated solely to maximising surpluses. Prestige and social standing are still important to universities and their staff and students. Universities may limit the number of students they accept to maintain standards and exclusivity.

A real free market would also allow HE institutions to offer a wide range of programmes, courses, and subjects. Although many new programmes have been created under current regulations, there are distinct limits. Moore (2021) stressed that no such market was created, and the price cannot signal the product's value:

> The £9,000 fee was intended as a maximum, to be charged in "exceptional circumstances", as the government put it at the time. It was expected that leaner, hungrier institutions would offer lower fees in order to compete on price. In the event, £9,000 turned out to be the almost universal standard rate, the minimum as well as the maximum, as few wanted to be the outfit selling cut-price and therefore suspect degrees.

The fact that research and teaching are, in many cases, complementary and interwoven can make it difficult to isolate and price education. Marketisation would create a market in which providers would compete on price. A more significant change in 2015 was the removal of the cap on undergraduate student numbers, which had been imposed until then. This change has allowed universities to recruit as many undergraduates as they would like. It opens up the demand side of the HE market, which was previously artificially limited. Since then, marketing and market positionality (in which student numbers are of great importance) have become much more important in the university's strategy and governance. Education is more manifested in policy intention than in reality. The theoretical "neoliberal market model for HE" (Marginson, 2013) is based on the assumption that the market is the most effective and efficient distributor of goods and services (Agasisti & Catalano, 2006; Brown, 2013; Lynch, 2006; Newman & Jahdi, 2009). Given its emphasis on informed choice and incentivised and a quasi-market between institutions intending to use the price mechanism, neoliberalism as a policy seems most applicable to these changes. In its insistence that students should be treated as HE market actors above any other type of engagement, the state's policy simultaneously adheres to neoliberalism as an ideological approach.

Private Good

As we saw in the previous chapter, neoliberalism tends to position education as a private good. Brown (2011, p. 119) argued that neoliberalism demands that formerly public goods should be "marketed and priced as individual consumer rather than public goods. Thus do toll roads and fee-per-use transport, school voucher programmes and high tuition institutions replace publicly funded transportation infrastructure and public education". A key question is whether HE can be considered a private good for which the free market would be appropriate. Scott (2016, p. 17) highlighted that private benefits and public benefits are hard to disentangle, and the balance between the two is volatile, variable, and hard to measure. From an economic perspective, private goods need to be rival and excludable, including their benefits. There are clear limits to who can participate, so HE is a rival good. The number of students who can participate can also easily be limited through entrance criteria and tuition fees, so it is an excludable good. Its benefits are not entirely private positive externalities, both economic and non-economic (Willetts, 2017). For instance, the knowledge generated within HE institutions is still widely regarded as conferring benefits to society. Here, we can see a distinct departure from neoliberal principles.

Quasi-Markets

In most major education systems, research and teaching are at least partly financed by the state, mixing market and non-market. The state also sets requirements for entering the market. England is a 'regulated quasi-market' (Le Grand & Bartlett, 1993; Agasisti & Catalano, 2006), in which competition is stimulated, particularly competition for research funds and within the postgraduate education market. Furthermore, HE institutions are nonprofit organisations, so they act differently from market actors in a free market. Yet certain features have to be in place to make the market competition work, including reliable market information, state regulation of prices, and quality in the institutions.

Market levers have been introduced, but market behaviour differs from that of those operating in a free market. According to Marginson (2013, p. 355), the neoliberal market model-oriented policy reform has failed. The idea was that HE would be produced as commodities subject to buyer-seller relations, in markets with free entry, by competing institutions/firms financed by shareholder equity, and committed to profit making and expansion of market share, with no government interference. Universities, in practice, are quite different from most free-market actors. HE cannot have capitalist markets (see also Brown, 2011a; Marginson, 2013; Hemsley-Brown, 2011; Agasisti & Catalano, 2006). The HE market would look quite different if it were free of regulation, barriers to market entry, and limits to tuition fees. Consumers would have no restrictions on what and where they can study.

What does a quasi-market setup mean for our assessment of neoliberalisation? The lack of free markets is not necessarily a fundamental issue for neoliberalism if the market mechanism can be extended. Yet, the fact is that marketisation policy is not actively looking to create a free market. Education as a good does not fit neatly with how we theoretically think about free markets. It is difficult to price, as its value can only be defined over the long term. Academic qualifications must be earned and cannot be directly sold to anyone who would like to buy one, irrespective of how much they are willing to pay (Scott, 2016, pp. 20–21).

Another issue is whether HE markets are created according to neoliberal ideals. Birch (2017) contrasted the understanding of markets for neoliberalism with neoclassical economists for whom markets and competition are framed as a set of conditions to be fulfilled, including a large number of buyers and sellers. For neoliberals, markets constitute the subjective process of price discovery. They contain the mechanism for 'rational action' irrespective of the society markets they operate in. Birch (2017) described it as follows:

> Claiming that markets are price-generating mechanisms that provide information to market participants as long as participants are competing when they make their choices. If competition is restricted, then markets cannot function properly. Moreover, any restrictions on competition mean that individuals cannot make choices properly—because markets would not provide proper information—and, therefore, they cannot learn how to conduct themselves properly [...] As such, Dardot and Laval argue, this Austrian/neoliberal conception of markets entails "a process of self-formation of the economic subject" in which the "market process constructs its own subject". (Birch, 2017, pp. 40–41)

For neoliberals, market actors need to be transformed into entrepreneurs to know how best to achieve their goals through the price signals the market offers. The state should make sure individuals think and act as such, maximising their benefit from the market and being able to express their freedom. In the English undergraduate market, there is no price competition. The UK state persistently intervenes in the market based on what they feel students need, want, or should want (e.g. access, value for money, employability, etc.). As a result, a different type of subject is more likely to be created.

The Role of Competition

Rather than markets, competition may define the English HE system. Competition is, of course, closely related to markets. Marketisation in HE is also thought to lead to greater value for money for students and taxpayers, as institutions can compete on price due to the variability in tuition fees. Successful courses will be in greater demand from students, and courses below standard will be rejected by the consumer, lose revenue, and be forced to improve or leave the market. This was thought to enhance the sector's efficiency, quality, and flexibility (Watts, 2017). Competition for students is also believed to lead to superior responsiveness to the needs of students and to promote innovative educational approaches and methods to attract new customers. There is a clear expectation that competition will lead to quality improvements in government policy

> Competition between providers in any market incentivises them to raise their game, offering consumers a greater choice of more innovative and better quality products and services at a lower cost. Higher education is no exception. (DBIS, 2016, p. 8)

In the English context, competition between HE institutions has been woven into the education system. Likewise, institutions 'compete' for research funding in the presence of private provision in the sector. It is clear that this competition has increased in recent decades. As mentioned before, removing the student cap has led to growing competition to attract students. Competition for postgraduate students has also risen in recent years (Das, 2023).

Is It Neoliberal?

There are reasons to believe that neoliberalism has not necessarily played a role in the use of competition within the HE system. First of all, competition has always been a central characteristic of academia. HE institutions in the UK have always competed for research funds, scholarships, and students, long before the emergence of neoliberalism. However, it is true that institutional competition is increasingly understood within market terms. It is also true that universities have been introduced to a range of new forms of competition, but not all competition is market competition. Instead, state-led reforms only design specific forms of competition. In recent years, Conservative governments have made efforts to intervene in either supply or demand. Education Secretary Gavin Williams has criticised New Labour's political aim of 50% of young people participating in HE, as there is no economic need to do so (Adams, 2020a). Minister Michelle Donelan has criticised English universities for 'dumbing down' and "recruiting too many young people onto courses that do nothing to improve their life chances" (Adams, 2020b).

Frank et al. (2019) argued that after the Browne Review, real competition has been effectively removed. Before this, universities had a set number of places and would compete for the best students. By removing the cap, competition was killed, as universities could simply admit more and/or weaker students. The authors call this an example of markets without competition. This brings us to a wider point. The British government certainly wants competition, but not necessarily market competition. For example, competition for research funding through research councils or other funders is competitive through a contest model rather than a price mechanism. Likewise, ranking exercises and evaluation are influential, but they occur through methodologies designed to measure teaching quality (TEF) or research excellence (REF), which are not market-based competitions. In addition, many of these competitions are predominantly about status or esteem. These status competitions may be intended to drive performance/outputs/impact but, again, not within or through a market. Status differentiation between universities, at national and international levels, is an important means by which universities make claims that will be advantageous to them in competition for students and research funds. It is status differentiation, not market differentiation, that drives HE systems' hierarchical segmentation (Marginson, 2006; Pusser & Marginson, 2013). Indicators of esteem can be along the lines of what anthropologists call a 'prestige economy' (Blackmore & Kandiko, 2011), shaped by what a group of people prizes highly. Prestige economies exist outside of a market. Institutional status is not distributed through the market and occurs in a much wider field through a wide range of governmental policies, judgements, competitions, and assessments.

HE competition is, as Musselin (2018, pp. 677–678) explained, "not a competition for prices or for customers, but rather a competition for quality. Furthermore, it is no longer limited to individual scientists and their teams, and to countries, but also applies to HE institutions that adopted competitive strategies and became competitors themselves". Whereas, in theory, increased provider competition and greater consumer choice offer sector diversity and differentiation, in practice, the sector has not diversified itself to a large extent. As noted in the previous section, differentiation in fees has not occurred, whereas institutional status remains strong and, most importantly, solidified. A related issue with competition is that competition does not have a single meaning, and the oft-used neoclassical one builds on pure and perfect competition, which contrasts with the imperfect version found in reality (Callon, 2021, p. 39). The imperfect education market does not map neatly onto the neoliberal conceptions of competition (e.g. Stigler, 1957). Yet, market competition often relies on the state to enhance and regulate competition rather than remove itself, which aligns with neoliberalism. We can also clearly observe that the politics of competition and competitiveness rely on a state supporting the expansion of economic rationales in areas of life where we do not necessarily expect them.

Finance and Fees

Marketisation initiatives are supportive of the notion that those who use a good or service must pay for it, especially given the wide array of private benefits to HE, including higher wages, better job quality, and positive health effects (Willetts, 2017). Mass HE has led to an increasing cost burden on the taxpayer who is (or is thought to be) less willing or able to fund it. This is why private tuition fees often support marketised HE systems. In a free market, users would meet the cost of fees. Yet, in many countries, most first degrees are subsidised by the government, at least to some extent. Between 1962 and the 1990s, HE in Britain was effectively free. Subsidisation, in some cases, is linked to a fixed number of government-subsidised places. Where tuition fees are high, HE arguably becomes more of a private good. Students may feel that their education is an investment. Of course, for the neoliberal, high tuition fees are not an issue if they are an outcome of the market, and students paying for their education are also acceptable. Cooper (2020, p. 118) observed that the history of HE funding in the United States stays very close to how neoliberals such as Friedman and Becker have set it out. Neoliberals have advocated private over public deficit spending in relation to HE financing. Public investment crowds out consumer credit markets and leads to suboptimal investments.

Another relevant dimension in relation to tuition fees is whether students pay them upfront or will repay them in the future, often as a graduate tax. In the case of England, the repayment system is complicated.

Students are not required to pay tuition fees back if their earnings are below a certain threshold. In the English context, this means that many graduates are unlikely to pay back their student loans. However, this situation may change in the future. For students in England who began university in the 2023/24 academic year, the threshold was reduced from £27,200 to £25,000, and repayments were extended to 40 years, meaning many graduates will be repaying student loans into their 60s (Weale, 2022).

HE institutions in the English context are nonprofit organisations with charitable status. Their primary purpose in advancing education and research is to deliver a public benefit. Nonetheless, their finances are significant, especially when income and costs have become more volatile and institutions have become more focused on their financial sustainability. Successful recruitment has become vital for most universities to survive. Some universities have increased the number of programmes on offer, and part of their business model has been to seek growth in overseas student numbers. However, the profit motive for universities is often muted, as their relationship to the capitalist market is different. They may seek to maximise revenues but do not produce surplus value or profit for their shareholders (Marginson, 2013). They cannot function like private firms that collect capital and profit for their owners. Marginson (2013, p. 360) noted, "[T]he fact that few institutions are financed by private equity is a major constraint on capitalist development". Neoliberal ideology might position HE institutions as corporate actors and, as such, embrace corporate governance. Universities may feel that they need to treat students as customers and maximise income through students' tuition fees. This would explain the greater emphasis on attracting, retaining, and upholding their teaching reputation to survive within a competitive education market.

The justification for increased tuition fees rests on the now-accepted idea that graduate premia' in wages largely represent the investments made by those attending HE. Labour market outcomes constitute information signals on the investments students have made (Tholen, 2022). The HE sector is framed as the key facilitator of economic success and individual labour market opportunities. Increasing competition, choice, and personal responsibility are needed. For this reason, students' employability and labour market outcomes have been a key concern for those calling for further HE marketisation. The growing reliance on the 'consumer' to pay for their education can only be upheld if the return to education continues to be strong. Individual learners and institutions must take responsibility for individual labour market success. They will know best, based on market signals, what investments to make. Responsibility is closely related to neoliberalism as a govermentality approach. Not just the tuition fee levels resonate within neoliberalism, but also how it creates a neoliberal subject.

THE ROLE OF THE STATE

Neoliberalism has clear and distinct views on the role of the state and its responsibilities towards the free market. A neoliberal state is not a minimal state or the absence of government but actively promotes the market mechanism in all areas of society. According to Foucault, its government works "tirelessly to ensure that competition plays a 'regulatory role at every moment and every point in society', thereby promoting the 'general regulation of society by the market'" (2008, p. 145). For the neoliberal, the state's role in the marketised HE system is by no means to retreat.

Agasti and Catalano (2006, p. 248) distinguished the 'market' model, in which HE institutions (like corporate companies) set their own prices for their teaching and research services without public intervention, from the 'centralistic' model, in which the state finances and centrally controls education production and regulates university activities by determining the prices (tuition fees) and admission to academic courses. The authors rightly stated that most countries are somewhere in the middle of a "mixture of state regulation and autonomy of institutions", yet a marketised HE system in principle can be low on autonomy and high on state regulation.

In the English context, the case of neoliberal governance is not *framed* as the need for neoliberalisation. Yet a drive to create quasi-market and other forms of competition has radically altered the governance of HE (Doherty, 2007). Some justification for further marketisation is driven by economic narratives (Tholen, 2022). The drive for a global knowledge economy that has driven educational policy even has neoliberal tenets (Heller, 2016). It is assumed that within the knowledge-based economy, individuals need to invest in their education and employability to reap the rewards of the growing demand for skilled labour. Krause-Jensen and Garsten (2014, p. 1) observed that most educational reforms are driven by the need to achieve global competitiveness and adapt to the advent of the so-called 'knowledge economy'. The state has not held itself responsible for providing full employment since the decline of industrial capitalism. The individualisation of labour market success was further cemented in the narrative of the global knowledge-based economy (Brown & Lauder, 2001). The state did have a role to play in encouraging participation in HE. A highly skilled labour force would be an important condition to attract investment (alongside other factors, such as infrastructure). Within HE policy, we can see a strong reliance on the perceived realities of this global economy (Tholen, 2017; Brown et al., 2008; Brown et al., 2020). The policy focus on the expansion of HE participation underpins marketisation (Tholen, 2022) as part of an economic strategy and part of and shares characteristics with the neoliberal ideology. Here, the state is taking control of the growth and development of HE as part of a wider economic strategy that ultimately has to lead to economic growth and market competitiveness.

The UK government has also used its HE marketisation policy to improve social mobility (Tholen, 2022). Both Labour and Conservative governments in the last 20 years have aimed to increase access to higher education to provide access to professional and managerial jobs for those willing to invest in HE, especially those from disadvantaged backgrounds. Marketisation would guarantee its affordability. The removal of caps opens up further opportunities to fulfil the demand for HE. Yet here, we can see a clear move away from what we can call neoliberalism, which is not concerned with outcomes and inequality. For instance, for Hayek, different individuals are differently valued in the marketplace. Unequal outcomes are not problematic as social mobility is possible, and there are opportunities for individuals to learn and try again. Redistribution by the state disincentivises individuals from doing so (Stedman Jones, 2012, pp. 63–64). Therefore, there are limits to the extent to which we can call the role of the state in marketisation neoliberal. We certainly see a retreat from allocating public funding to support HE. Equally important, we can see greater control from the state over HE, specifically, interventions based on interpreting (labour market) outcomes. In other words, the state's control is used for a wider variety of purposes, not necessarily for the promotion of markets (e.g. widening participation). In fact, we have seen the role of the state increase and the independence of HE institutions be compromised.

Shattock and Horvath (2020) described the transformation from a self-governed to a regulated HE, which occurred predominantly after 1992. This governance of the HE system was increasingly driven by political and ideological underpinnings. Some of these regulations were meant to inject more markets into the system. The idea that policymakers can demand to intervene in the system has solidified. Whereas in the past, greater direction from the national government was associated with increased state funding (Naidoo & Williams, 2015), we now see a different dynamic in which the government implements a neoliberal policy approach in promoting markets while simultaneously moving away from where it decides to intervene or put pressures on universities or the sector as a whole. The state is constantly disturbing the market mechanism for various political reasons. In some cases, these are merely warnings or threats towards HE institutions. Others are supported by actual policies. Some examples from recent years are given below:

Free speech. In 2022, the HE minister commented on a report highlighting growth in support for censorship by students. Donelan states, "University leaders can no longer afford to stand aside, but must take active steps to combat these intolerant attitudes on campus, both promoting and protecting free speech" (Adams, 2022). In 2023, Rishi Sunak summoned university vice-chancellors to Downing Street to discuss how Jewish students can be protected on campus against antisemitic behaviour (Duncan, 2024). In 2023, the government introduced legislation forcing universities to protect and promote freedom of speech on campus (DfE, 2023b).

Migration. In 2023, former Minister of State for Universities, Science, Research, and Innovation Jo Johnson warned UK universities to urgently reduce the number of "fraudulent" applications from international students "or risk facing a backlash in Westminster" (Foster, 2023). In the same year, Home Office officials warned universities of the increase in foreign students seeking asylum within months of arriving in the UK (Henry, 2023). A group of Conservative MPs pushed the government to reduce the number of study visas by around 75,000 by excluding financially struggling universities from eligibility (Elsom, 2023).

Mental health. In 2018, the government issued an ultimatum to vice-chancellors to improve student mental health, warning them, "It is not good enough to suggest that university is about academic education and nothing else" (Weale, 2018). In 2023, Robert Halfon MP, Minister for State for Skills, Apprenticeships, and Higher Education, urged the universities to adopt the University Mental Health Charter Framework and set out stricter licensing conditions if they failed to comply: "if we do not see the expected improvements I will not hesitate to ask the Office for Students to introduce a new registration condition on mental health" (Perera, 2023).

Consumer protection. Plans for Ofsted-style rankings for English universities have also been developed. A key measure of quality would be graduate earnings, with courses associated with low earnings labelled as failing by the Office for Students. The Department for Education commented, "The government subsidises around 50% of the cost of HE and it is only fair that this funding is used as efficiently as possible, so students can be confident they are getting good value for money" (Fazackerley, 2023). In 2022, Minister for Higher and Further Education Michelle Donelan expressed the view that students unhappy with their courses should be able to apply for a refund of their tuition fees. She argued: "They are consumers, at the end of the day. They're paying a substantial amount of money that's an investment in their own lives. They deserve that appeal right" (Tominey, 2022). In 2022, Education Minister Nadhim Zahawi proposed a crackdown on 'Mickey Mouse' degrees by obliging universities to include the drop-out rate and graduate job outcomes on every degree. He compared this with the need for banks to be upfront about the annual percentage rate when they advertise financial loans (Mikhailova, 2022).

Access to HE. In 2022, Secretary of State for Education Michelle Donelan wanted to introduce minimum entry requirements to prevent students who do not pass English and maths GCSEs or have two Es in A-levels from accessing student loans. She justified this by stating that social mobility is not achieved by pushing young people into university (Adam & Weale, 2022). In 2019, Education Secretary Damian Hinds wanted universities to stop offering "conditional unconditional offers" by which a university guarantees a student a place regardless of A-level results, provided they choose the institution as their first option. According to Hinds, the practice is "damaging the global reputation of universities in England and may be in breach of consumer protection laws" (Weale, 2019).

Quality of teaching. Universities Minister Sam Gyimah warned universities of low-quality courses (expressed as low earnings after graduation). This was, in particular, an issue with rapidly increasing student numbers. He said, "How do you deal with class sizes, how do you deal with lectures, when you're expanding this much?" (Busby, 2018). Michelle Donelan, in 2022, also announced a purge of bad quality HE courses as part of her goal to "revolutionise" higher education, ensuring that every young person has a range of "high-quality" routes available to them. Measures would include "[T]argeted limits on low-quality courses, to prevent courses that are known to be of low quality from procreating" (Wingate, 2022).

We can see increasing bureaucracy, a reduction in autonomy, and a growing sense that it is justified to meddle with how universities are run, what they do, and how they do it. This type of intervention would represent an overreach of government for neoliberals, as it does not benefit the market (or benefit law and order) and would most likely lead to inefficiencies and loss of freedom. The government seemingly tries to widen its interests to the detriment of the market. Perhaps a neoliberal state should not be expected any time soon. Bowl et al. (2018, p. 6) remind us that free-market HE systems are undesirable to governments that want to "maintain some control over the supply of university places, the costs of university study, who studies what and for what future purpose. They will also wish to promote their own social policies through HE".

Thus, HE policy may not be as neoliberal as many assume it is. Some have argued that marketisation policies were primarily driven by often pragmatic public finance concerns and not by a neoliberal policy drive. Hillman (2016) discussed the increase in tuition fees in England:

> First, the primary goal of the increase in tuition fees was to ensure the Business, Innovation, and Skills Department, which had an unprotected budget, contributed sufficiently to the planned reduction in the deficit [...] For Conservative Ministers, the fact that higher fees could make higher education more like a regulated market, with students coming to resemble consumers, was a bonus, but it was not the primary purpose.

Universities

Has marketisation changed universities into neoliberal institutions? Or did neoliberal universities implement marketisation because of their belief in competition and the free market? The idea that institutions have moved closer to the market and, as a result, are willing to adopt objectives and values and develop processes to be found in the private sector is not unreasonable. With universities in the English context more reliant on non-government funding, universities have become more attuned to markets in terms of students and research since the increase in undergraduate tuition fees. Universities face stronger incentives to embrace markets forced or made possible by external forces. The globalisation of HE, in particular, has incentivised marketisation for many universities in both research and education. The strongest global research universities have seen their income grow along with the maintenance of their status, as their brand value underpins their status and profits. However, status and market positioning interact in complex ways (Marginson, 2017, p. 365).

The demand that universities act like businesses and private sector corporations was first made in the Jarrat Report in 1985. From that point onwards, growing marketisation shaped how universities operated. Twenty-five years ago, Marginson (1999, cited in Olssen & Peters, 2005, p. 327) observed market-driven organisational changes, including the following:

- The rise of flexible executive-directed systems for internal university consultation and communication, from internal market research to vice-chancellors' advisory groups.
- The removal from the collegial view of key decisions regarding governance.
- Research management is subject to homogenising systems for assessing performance.
- The prioritisation of research in terms of quantity of research income rather than in terms of the number of publications produced or the quality of scholarship.

Commercialisation, enterprise, and corporate partnerships have intensified in university research in the last decades (Feola et al., 2021; Parker, 2022). The government still funds about half of UK universities/research income (UKRI, 2023).

Audit Practices

With marketisation, new techniques of quality and performance measurement arrive to make direct comparisons between institutions possible. These tend to focus on systems of classifications, such as 'league' tables, which promote and strengthen competition for status, resources, and students between students and the search for prestige and distinction. In 1985, the Jarratt Report examined how universities, as corporate enterprises, could increase 'value for money' and 'efficiency'. It proposed the adoption of 'performance indicators' to improve efficiency through competition and internal markets. Since then, an increasing number of assessments have been implemented. The Research Assessment Exercise (RAE) (known as the Research Excellence Framework (REF) since 2007) was created to assess the quality of research at universities. Since 1993, teaching quality has been evaluated through what has become known as the Teaching Quality Assessment. After 2017, the Teaching Excellence and

Student Outcomes Framework (TEF) came into being. It assesses universities on the quality of the student experience, teaching standards, and labour market outcomes for graduates. It includes the number of contact hours students receive and the class sizes in which they are taught. In the education market, TEF assessment outcomes were expected to signal teaching quality and to show greater demand for those courses and universities that performed well. Courses that could not raise standards or differentiate themselves in the sector would eventually withdraw.

Rankings have been fundamental in how modern universities behave (Dill & Soo, 2005; Hazelkorn, 2015; Lynch, 2006; Pusser & Marginson, 2013). The quality criteria used by these ranking exercises have become a means in themselves, and institutions worldwide can be compared to influence the behaviour towards these achievements with relative lowering of priority of other areas. Universities themselves start to see their objectives in relation to ranking and audit exercises. The need for transparency is only partially driven by 'consumers' of HE needs—but equally by universities' natural drive for prestige and status within a heterogeneous university sector (Marginson, 2006, 2008). Audit culture clashes with the previous conceptualisation of a university around the autonomy and independence of institutions. Maybe for this reason, it has been met with significant protest as it inserts "market values into organisations that are not appropriate, that divert or undermine the values the organisation is supposed to uphold" (Nash, 2019, p. 179).

According to Gane (2012), neoliberalism is expressed in the audit culture in which universities actively surveil themselves with the state, setting the conditions and parameters for this artificially induced competition. Audit exercises, such as the REF, "work to promote competition in ways that were previously unimaginable" (Gane, 2012, p. 629). Gane convincingly argued that Foucault's work on governmentality provides insights regarding these forms of surveillance often directed by the state. He stated that HE institutions need to

> show 'permanent vigilance, activity, and intervention' (Foucault, 2008, p. 132) through processes of self-surveillance and intervention or what might be called audit to promote competition, and thereby to achieve legitimacy in the face of the market [...] In these terms, it is possible to explain the ongoing drive for measurement, audit and classification within the state and public sector institutions more generally: they are there to manufacture marketized forms of competition where previously they did not exist. (Gane, 2012, pp. 631–632)

The importance of entrepreneurialism for the modern academic matches neoliberalism's conception of the individual. The individual within the market is seen as an innovator and exploiter of opportunities. Academics dealing with the marketised HE are shaped by a neoliberal rationale, which "produces the subject it requires by deploying the means of governing him so that he really does conduct himself as an entity in a competition, who must maximise his result by exposing himself to risks and taking responsibility for possible failures" (Dardot & Laval, 2013, p. 261). The ubiquitous metric performance systems may help underpin such a neoliberal rationality.

Managerialism

As we saw in the previous chapter, managerialism in HE is often aligned with neoliberal dominance in academia. It is important to note that managerial governance does not necessarily lead to market rule (Knafo et al., 2019), and the relationship between managerialism and marketisation is not straightforward. The dominance of the interests of managers in shaping how organisations should be run can lead to a variety of outcomes that are not necessarily in line with the free market. The adoption of a more business-like approach and private sector practices has had a significant impact on HE. HE institutions mimic management approaches from the private sector, as though their institutions were in a free market in which profit motive and efficiencies are defined by market parameters called 'quasi-markets'.

How managerialism as part of marketisation relates to neoliberalism is delicate (Knafo et al., 2019). Neoliberal ideas about the role of markets and competition are not necessarily linked to the drive for greater managerialism in organisations, including HE institutions. Management also does not receive much attention in the works of neoliberal authors, such as Hayek and Friedman.

The most promising way managerialism in HE can connect with neoliberalism is through neoliberal governmentality, in particular, where it concerns accountability and performance drive, which often defines the managerialism seen in HE. Academics now self-govern based on the managerial principles that drive the technologies of the self that enlist academics in their own governance (Shields & Watermeyer, 2020). Effort, values, purposes, and self-understanding in universities are now all shaped according to external measures and comparisons, according to Ball (2003, 2012).

This leads to misrepresentation and devaluation of the meaning of academic work. Academics are morally subjected to the performance system, which affects the academic sense of personal worth.

Students

The change from the student as a person with rights to education to being positioned as a customer with preferences presents a massive shift in how HE is understood (Lolich, 2011). It is not unreasonable to think that as students become market actors buying what universities offer, they become foremost consumers in a commodified system. A broad body of literature has assumed that as consumers, students are treated, and understand themselves, as market actors. Some scholars have seen consumerism as an intrinsic part of neoliberal HE (Naidoo & Jamieson, 2005; Naidoo et al., 2011). For instance, the dominant marketing approach to student recruitment highlights individual choice-making on the part of potential students and their families 'as if' HE were a free market. Vocabularies consistent with market practices turn the student into a customer or client who should have consumer choice.

For many, the instrumental rationalised institutions that actively focus on the student experience are evidence of neoliberal-style consumerism, in which the students are active market participants making choices from the educational options available in the marketplace. The positioning of students as consumers and their expected rational behaviour drive the need for further transparency and more detailed information so that students can make sound decisions in the marketplace. Have students therefore become neoliberal agents? There is evidence to suggest that commodification impacts the student experience and students' understanding of HE and themselves as learners (Bunce et al., 2017; Nixon et al., 2018). There is also evidence to suggest that students do not necessarily think like consumers (Tomlinson, 2017; McCulloch, 2009; Jones et al., 2020), or students actively resist being consumers (Brooks et al., 2016).

Competition among students to gain places in the most sought-after universities has been part of HE for a very long time. Yet it is fair to say that the student is now positioned by universities and the state as consumers, as though part of a free market in HE. For example, take the HE regulator, the Office for Students (OfS), created after the Higher Education and Research Act in 2017 to regulate the new student market and oversee whether competition and choice are expressed in the system. As the name suggests, it primarily defends the interest of the student, who is thought to benefit from greater choice and competition. As such, it is in line with the policy approach to neoliberalism, which aims to introduce competition throughout society as a policy aim. Yet, at the same time, it offers market protection. The OfS is not simply a regulator but is open to intervening beyond market regulation (Shattock & Horvath, 2020, p. 36). Unlike many other regulators, it actively intervenes in the market in the interest of consumers to improve what they understand as quality and promotes value for money in the provision of HE by English providers. It is driven to improve the market for HE. For instance, it aims to protect students from grade inflation (PA Media, 2022). In addition, it takes into account the interests of the taxpayers, who "receive value for money when HE providers use public money and students fees efficiently and effectively to deliver graduates, from all backgrounds, who contribute to society and the economy" (OfS, 2019, p. 4). The policy drive that makes students responsible for their choices and promotes the virtue of markets as benefitting students (as well as employers and taxpayers) is solidified in the regulatory framework that the UK government has set up for the English HE system.

CONCLUSION

Marketisation has undoubtedly changed HE in the UK. This chapter examined how well marketisation in the UK context fits a neoliberal blueprint. The evidence for neoliberalism to be the driver of marketisation is mixed. It would not be justified to characterise the growing marketisation as neoliberalism in action *pur sang*. However, the chapter identified areas where neoliberalism as a concept could be insightful. This would depend on more than one definition of neoliberalism. Table 5.1 shows which approach is best suited for understanding the different dimensions of marketisation. It is important not to essentialise these. As we have seen, more than one approach may fit an aspect of marketisation. Yet, at the very minimum, a more focused understanding of neoliberalisation allows us to think more critically about whether the underlying processes represent a form of neoliberalism.

Table 5.1 Dimension of marketisation and forms of neoliberalism

Dimension of marketisation	Neoliberalism as policy	Neoliberalism as ideology	Neoliberalism as governmentality
1. Market		X	
2. Competition	X	X	
3. Finance		X	X
4. State	X		
5. University			
Audit culture			X
Managerialism			X
Students	X		

Note

1. The number of government-subsidised places is normally fixed (Scotland) in contrary to demand-driven systems.

References

Adam, R., & Weale, S. (2022). Ministers' loan plans could stop poorer students in England going to university. *The Guardian*, February 22. Retrieved April 24, 2024, from https://www.theguardian.com/education/2022/feb/22/fears-that-minimum-grades-for-student-loans-in-england-could-narrow-access

Adams, R. (2020a). Ministers to ditch target of 50% of young people in England going to university. *The Guardian*, July 9. Retrieved April 24, 2024, from https://www.theguardian.com/politics/2020/jul/09/ministers-to-ditch-target-of-50-of-young-people-in-england-going-to-university

Adams, R. (2020b). Minister lambasts English universities for letting down students. *The Guardian*, July 1. Retrieved April 24, 2024, from https://www.theguardian.com/education/2020/jul/01/minister-lambasts-uk-universities-policy-for-letting-down-students

Adams, R. (2022). Students show 'shocking growth in support for censorship', ministers warn. *The Guardian*, June 23. Retrieved April 24, 2024, from https://www.theguardian.com/education/2022/jun/23/students-shocking-growth-support-censorship-ministers-warn

Agasisti, T., & Catalano, G. (2006). Governance models of university systems – towards quasi-markets? Tendencies and perspectives: A European comparison. *Journal of Higher Education Policy and Management, 28*(3), 245–262.

Ball, S. J. (2003). The teacher's soul and the terrors of performativity. *Journal of Education Policy, 18*(2), 215–228.

Ball, S. J. (2012). Performativity, commodification, and commitment: An I-Spy guide to the neoliberal university. *British Journal of Educational Studies*, 60(1), 17–28.

Biebrichter, T. (2018). *The Political Theory of Neoliberalism*. Stanford University Press.

Birch, K. (2017). *A Research Agenda for Neoliberalism*. Edward Elgar.

Blackmore, P., & Kandiko, C. B. (2011). Motivation in academic life: A prestige economy. *Research in Post-Compulsory Education*, 16(4), 399–411.

Bok, D. (2003). *Universities in the Marketplace: The Commercialization of Higher Education*. Princeton University Press.

Bolton, P. (2024). Research briefing house of commons library. *Higher Education Student Numbers*, January 2. Retrieved April 24, 2024, from https://commonslibrary.parliament.uk/research-briefings/cbp-7857/

Bowl, M. (2018). Diversity and differentiation, equity and equality in a marketised higher education system. In M. Bowl, C. McCaig, & J. Hughes (Eds.), *Equality and Differentiation in Marketised Higher Education. Palgrave Studies in Excellence and Equity in Global Education* (pp. 1–20). Palgrave Macmillan.

Brooks, R., Byford, K., & Sela, K. (2016). Students' unions, consumerism and the neo-liberal university. *British Journal of Sociology of Education*, 37(8), 1–19.

Brown, W. (2011). Neoliberalized knowledge. *History of the Present*, 1(1), 113–129.

Brown, R. (Ed.). (2011a). *Higher Education and the Market*. Routledge.

Brown, R. (2011b). The impact of markets. In R. Brown (Ed.), *Higher Education and the Market* (pp. 20–52). Routledge.

Brown, R. (2013). *Everything for Sale? The Marketization of UK Higher Education*. Routledge.

Brown, P., & Lauder, H. (2001). *Capitalism and Social Progress: The Future of Society in a Global Economy*. Palgrave.

Brown, P., Lauder, H., Ashton, D., Yingje, W., & Vincent-Lancrin, S. (2008). Education, globalisation and the future of the knowledge economy. *European Educational Research Journal*, 7(2), 131–156.

Brown, P., H. Lauder, H. & S.Y. Cheung. (2020). *The Death of Human Capital: Its Failed Promise and How to Renew it*. Oxford University Press.

Brown, R., & Scott, P. (2009). The role of the market in higher education. Retrieved April 24, 2024, from https://www.hepi.ac.uk/2009/03/18/the-role-of-the-market-in-higher-education/

Bunce, L., Baird, A., & Jones, S. E. (2017). The student as consumer approach in higher education and its effects on academic performance. *Studies in Higher Education*, 2(11), 1958–1978.

Busby, E. (2018). Minister criticises universities so overcrowded students 'forced to stand at back of lecture halls without desk'. *The Independent*, June 7. Retrieved April 24, 2024, from https://www.independent.co.uk/news/education/education-news/students-universities-sam-gyimah-vice-chancellors-tuition-fees-graduate-earnings-lecture-halls-a8387701.html

Callon, M. (2021). *Markets in the Making: Rethinking Competition, Goods, and Innovation.* Zone Books.

Cooper, M. (2020). Neoliberalism's family values: Welfare, human capital, and kinship. In P. Mirowski, D. Plehwe, & Q. Slobodian (Eds.), *Nine Lives of Neoliberalism* (pp. 95–119). Verso Books.

Dardot, P., & Laval, C. (2013). *The New Way of the World: On Neoliberal Society.* Verso books.

Das, S. (2023). UK universities paying millions in agent fees to secure international students. *The Guardian*, November 18. Retrieved April 24, 2024, from https://www.theguardian.com/education/2023/nov/18/uk-universities-paying-millions-in-agent-fees-to-secure-international-students

Department for Business, Innovation and Skills. (2015). *Fulfilling Our Potential: Teaching Excellence, Social Mobility and Student Choice.* HM Government.

Department for Business, Innovation and Skills (DBIS). (2011). *Students at the Heart of the System.* DBIS.

Department for Business Innovation and Skills (DBIS). (2016). *Success as a Knowledge Economy: Teaching Excellence, Social Mobility and Student Choice.* HM Government.

Department for Education (DfE). (2023a). Crackdown on rip-off university degrees. Retrieved April 24, 2024, from https://www.gov.uk/government/news/crackdown-on-rip-off-university-degrees

Department for Education (DfE). (2023b). University freedom of speech bill becomes law. Retrieved April 24, 2024, from https://www.gov.uk/government/news/university-freedom-of-speech-bill-becomes-law

Dill, D. D. (1997). Higher education markets and public policy. *Higher Education Policy, 10*(3), 167–185.

Dill, D. D. (2003). Allowing the market to rule: The case of the United States. *Higher Education Quarterly, 57*(2), 136–157.

Dill, D. D., & Soo, M. (2005). Academic quality, league tables, and public policy: A cross-national analysis of university ranking systems. *Higher Education, 49*(4), 495–533.

Doherty, R. A. (2007). Education, neoliberalism and the consumer citizen: After the golden age of egalitarian reform. *Critical Studies in Education, 48*(2), 269–288.

Duncan, G. (2024). Rishi Sunak summons university leaders after warning UK is descending into 'mob rule. *The National News*, February 29. Retrieved April 24, 2024, from https://www.thenationalnews.com/world/uk-news/2024/02/29/rishi-sunak-calls-in-university-leaders-after-warning-uk-is-descending-into-mob-rule/

Elsom, J. (2023). Course of action slashing immigration must come before propping up 'failing' universities, Tories warn. *The Sun*, July 3. Retrieved April 24, 2024, from https://www.thesun.co.uk/news/politics/22912345/slashing-immigration-must-come-before-unis/

Fazackerley, A. (2023). Top universities 'will turn away more UK students' as fees fail to match costs. *The Guardian*, July 29. Retrieved April 24, 2024, from https://www.theguardian.com/education/2023/jul/29/top-universities-will-turn-away-more-uk-students-as-fees-fail-to-match-costs

Feola, R., Parente, R., & Cucino, V. (2021). The entrepreneurial university: How to develop the entrepreneurial orientation of academia. *Journal of the Knowledge Economy, 12*(4), 1787–1808.

Foster, P. (2023). UK universities urged to cut 'fraudulent' international student applications. *Financial Times*, October 19. Retrieved April 24, 2024, from https://www.ft.com/content/d60acbb1-49cc-4a3f-805a-4cee6c320370

Foucault, M. (2008). *The Birth of Biopolitics: Lectures at the Collège de France, 1978–79*. Palgrave.

Frank, J., Gowar, N., & Naef, M. (2019). *English Universities in Crisis: Markets without Competition*. Bristol University Press.

Gane, N. (2012). The governmentalities of neoliberalism: Panopticism, post-panopticism and beyond. *The Sociological Review, 60*(4), 611–634.

Hayek, F. (1945). The use of knowledge in society. *American Economic Review, 35*(4), 519–530.

Hazelkorn, E. (2015). *Rankings and the Reshaping of Higher Education: The Battle for World-Class Excellence* (2nd ed.). Palgrave Macmillan.

Heller, H. (2016). *The Capitalist University: The Transformations of Higher Education in the United States since 1945*. Pluto Press.

Hemsley-Brown, J. (2011). Market heal thyself: The challenges of a free market in higher education. *Journal of Marketing for Higher Education, 21*(2), 115–132.

Henkel, M. (1997). Academic values and the university as corporate enterprise. *Higher Education Quarterly, 51*(2), 134–143.

Henry, J. (2023). Immigration chiefs warn universities after thousands of foreign students claim asylum within months of arriving in Britain. *Daily Mail*, October 28. Retrieved April 24, 2024, from https://www.dailymail.co.uk/news/article-12683921/Immigration-chiefs-warn-universities-thousands-foreign-students-claim-asylum-months-arriving-Britain.html

Hillman, N. (2016). The coalition's higher education reforms in England. *Oxford Review of Education, 42*(3), 330–345.

HM Government. (2004). *Higher Education Act*. HMSO.

Hunt, S. A., & Boliver, V. (2023). The private higher education provider landscape in the UK. *Studies in Higher Education, 48*(9), 1346–1360.

Jones, S., Vigurs, K., & Harris, D. (2020). Discursive framings of market-based education policy and their negotiation by students: the case of 'value for money' in English universities. *Oxford Review of Education, 46*(3), 375–392.

Jongbloed, B. (2003). Marketisation in higher education, Clark's triangle and the essential ingredients of markets. *Higher Education Quarterly, 57*(2), 110–135.

Knafo, S., Dutta, S. J., Lane, R., Wyn-Jones, S., & S. (2019). The managerial lineages of neoliberalism. *New Political Economy, 24*(2), 235–251.

Komljenovic, J. (2020). Commodifying higher education: The proliferation of devices for making markets. In C. Callender, W. Locke, & S. Marginson (Eds.), *Changing Higher Education for a Changing World* (pp. 191–204). Bloomsbury.

Krause-Jenson, J., & Garsten, C. (2014). Introduction: Neoliberal turns in higher education. *Learning and Teaching, 7*(3), 1–13.

Le Grand, J., & Bartlett, W. (1993). *Quasi-markets and Social Policy.* Macmillan.

Lolich, L. (2011). ...and the market created the student to its image and likening. Neo-liberal governmentality and its effects on higher education in Ireland. *Irish Educational Studies, 30*(2), 271–284.

Lynch, K. (2006). Neo-liberalism and marketisation: The implications for higher education. *European Educational Research Journal, 5*(1), 1–17.

Marginson, S. (2006). Dynamics of national and global competition in higher education. *Higher Education, 52*(1), 1–39.

Marginson, S. (2008). Global field and global imagining: Bourdieu and worldwide higher education. *British Journal of Sociology of Education, 29*(3), 303–315.

Marginson, S. (2013). The impossibility of capitalist markets in higher education. *Journal of Education Policy, 28*(3), 353–370.

Marginson, S. (2017). The World-Class Multiversity: Global commonalities and national characteristics. *Frontiers of Education in China, 12,* 233–260.

McCulloch, A. (2009). The student as co-producer: Learning from public administration about the student-university relationship. *Studies in Higher Education, 34*(2), 171–183.

McGettigan, A. (2013). *The Great University Gamble: Money, Markets and the Future of Higher Education.* Pluto Press.

Mikhailova, A. (2022). Education secretary Nadhim Zahawi plans crackdown on 'Mickey Mouse' degrees – with universities required to publish drop-out rate and graduate job outcomes on every advert *Daily Mail*, March 20. Retrieved April 24, 2024, from https://www.dailymail.co.uk/news/article-10631871/Education-Secretary-Nadhim-Zahawi-plans-crackdown-Mickey-Mouse-degrees.html

Molesworth, M., Scullion, R., & Nixon, E. (Eds.). (2010). *The Marketisation of Higher Education: The Student as Consumer.* Routledge.

Moore, R. 2021. The free-market gamble: Has Covid broken UK universities? *The Guardian*, January 17. Retrieved April 24, 2024, from https://www.theguardian.com/education/2021/jan/17/free-market-gamble-has-covid-broken-uk-universities

Morgan, H. (2022). Neoliberalism's influence on American universities: How the business model harms students and society. *Policy Futures in Education, 20*(2), 149–165.

Musselin, C. (2018). New forms of competition in higher education. *Socio-Economic Review, 16*(3), 657–683.

Naidoo, R., & Jamieson, I. (2005). Empowering participants or corroding learning: Towards a research agenda on the impact of student consumerism in higher education. *Journal of Education Policy, 20*(3), 267–281.

Naidoo, R., Shankar, A., & Veer, E. (2011). The consumerist turn in higher education: Policy aspirations and outcomes. *Journal of Marketing Management, 27*(11–12), 1142–1162.

Naidoo, R., & Williams, J. (2015). The neoliberal regime in English higher education: Charters, consumers and the erosion of the public good. *Critical Studies in Education, 56*(2), 208–223.

Nash, K. (2019). Neo-liberalisation, universities and the values of bureaucracy. *The Sociological Review, 67*(1), 178–193.

Newman, S., & Jahdi, K. (2009). Marketisation of education: Marketing, rhetoric and reality. *Journal of Further and Higher Education, 33*(1), 1–11.

Nixon, E., Scullion, R., & Hearn, R. (2018). Her majesty the student: Marketised higher education and the narcissistic (dis)satisfactions of the student-consumer. *Studies in Higher Education, 43*(6), 927–943.

Office for Students (OfS). (2019). Office for Students' value for money strategy 2019 to 2021. Retrieved April 24, 2024, from https://www.officeforstudents.org.uk/media/336c258b-d94c-4f15-af0a-42e1be8f66a1/ofs-vfm-strategy.pdf

Olssen, M., & Peters, M. A. (2005). Neoliberalism, higher education and the knowledge economy: From the free market to knowledge capitalism. *Journal of Education Policy, 20*(3), 313–345.

PA media. (2022). Sharp rise in top degrees at three English universities investigated. *The Guardian*, September 2. Retrieved April 24, 2024, from https://www.theguardian.com/education/2022/sep/02/office-for-students-investigates-sharp-rise-top-degrees-universities

Parker, L. D. (2022). Public university research engagement contradictions in a commercialisation higher education world. *Financial Accountability & Management, 40*(1), 1–18.

Perera, M. (2023). Minister asks universities to adopt mental health charter by September 2024 or face licensing restrictions. *Epigram*, June 12. Retrieved April 24, 2024, from https://epigram.org.uk/minister-asks-universities-to-adopt-mental-health-charter-by-september-2024-or-face-licensing-restrictions/

Pusser, B., & Marginson, S. (2013). University rankings in critical perspective. *Higher Education, 84*(4), 544–568.

Scott, P. (2016). Private commodities and public goods: Markets and values in higher education. In P. John & J. Fanghanel (Eds.), *Dimensions of Marketisation in Higher Education* (pp. 15–25). Routledge.

Shattock, M., & Horvath, A. (2020). *The Governance of British Higher Education the Impact of Governmental, Financial and Market Pressures*. Bloomsbury.

Shields, R., & Watermeyer, R. (2020). Competing institutional logics in universities in the United Kingdom: Schism in the church of reason. *Studies in Higher Education, 45*(1), 3–17.

Stedman Jones, D. (2012). *Masters of the Universe Hayek, Friedman, and the Birth of Neoliberal Politics*. Princeton University Press.

Stigler, G. (1957). Perfect competition, historically contemplated. *The Journal of Political Economy, 65*(1), 1–17.

Tholen, G. (2017). *Graduate Work: Skills, Credentials, Careers, and Labour Markets*. Oxford University Press.

Tholen, G. (2022). *Modern Work and the Marketisation of Higher Education*. Policy Press.

Tominey, C. (2022). 'Students should apply for refunds on their fees – at the end of the day, they're consumers'. *The Telegraph*, January 21. Retrieved April 24, 2024, from https://www.telegraph.co.uk/education-and-careers/2022/01/21/students-should-apply-refunds-fees-end-day-consumers/

Tomlinson, M. (2017). Student perceptions of themselves as 'consumers' of higher education, British. *Journal of Sociology of Education, 38*(4), 450–467.

UK Research and Innovation (UKRI). (2023). Research financial sustainability. https://www.ukri.org/publications/research-financial-sustainability-data/research-financial-sustainability-issues-paper/.

Watts, R. (2017). *Public Universities, Managerialism and the Value of Higher Education*. Palgrave Macmillan.

Weale, S. (2018). Student mental health must be top priority – universities minister. *The Guardian*, June 28. Retrieved April 24, 2024, from https://www.theguardian.com/education/2018/jun/28/student-mental-health-must-be-top-priority-universities-minister

Weale, S. (2019). DfE tells universities to stop 'unethical' admissions tactics. *The Guardian*, April 5. Retrieved April 24, 2024, from https://www.theguardian.com/education/2019/apr/05/dfe-tells-universities-to-stop-unethical-admissions-tactics

Weale, S. (2022). Students in England to pay back loans over 40 years instead of 30. *The Guardian*, February 24. Retrieved April 24, 2024, from https://www.theguardian.com/money/2022/feb/24/students-in-england-to-pay-back-loans-over-40-years-instead-of-30

Weale, S. (2023). Minister rules out lifting cap on student tuition fees in England. *The Guardian*, August 2. Retrieved April 24, 2024, from https://www.theguardian.com/education/2023/aug/02/minister-rules-out-lifting-cap-on-student-tuition-fees-in-england

Willetts, D. (2017). *A University Education*. Oxford University Press.

Williams, G. (1997). The market route to mass higher education: British experience 1979–1996. *Higher Education Policy, 10*(3–4), 275–289.

Williams, J. (2013). *Consuming Higher Education: Why Learning can't be Bought.* Bloomsbury.

Wingate, S. (2022). Universities should limit 'low-quality' courses, minister says. *The Independent*, June 9. Retrieved April 24, 2024, from https://www.independent.co.uk/news/uk/universities-hepi-mental-health-nottingham-trent-university-government-b2097425.html

CHAPTER 6

Conclusion

Abstract This is the final chapter of the book and looks back at the question of how and to what extent the concept of neoliberalism can be used to understand marketisation in HE. It argues that there is scope for the use of the concept of neoliberalism, but it will not be applicable in all areas. Also, at least three distinct approaches to the concept of neoliberalism can be used to understand more specifically the role of neoliberalism. This chapter reflects on what these arguments mean for our understanding of marketisation and neoliberalism. The chapter ends with an alternative framing of the role of neoliberalism in HE, which draws on wider changes in society's understanding of the purpose of universities.

Keywords Neoliberalism • Marketisation • Higher Education

INTRODUCTION

Today, 'globalisation' remains one of the most overused concepts in the social sciences and within the popular domain. Although there is no lack of definitions (Michie, 2019), it has been used in a wide range of ways in the last 30 years, so much so that its heuristic power is severely diminished.

© The Author(s), under exclusive license to Springer Nature
Switzerland AG 2024
G. Tholen, *The Role of Neoliberalism in the Marketisation of Higher Education*, Palgrave Studies on Global Policy and Critical Futures in Education, https://doi.org/10.1007/978-3-031-66281-2_6

The concept of 'neoliberalism' seems destined for the same fate. The overuse and misuse of the concept of neoliberalism have impacted its value within the social sciences. Too often, it is used to mean 'contemporary' ('in neoliberal times') or to signify an evil or damaging force within the social, economic, or political domains. For most, it has a more specific meaning, but there is no agreement on what falls inside or outside the concept; thus, it becomes possible to include a wide range of ideas within the neoliberal category. As Peck et al. (2018, p. 3) observed, "the 'flexible credo' of neoliberalism has been realised through a somewhat improvised and shape-shifting repertoire of pro-corporate, pro-market programs, projects, and power-plays".

As outlined in Chap. 2, the intellectual history of neoliberalism deals with a wide range of ideas but is linked to a relatively small number of economists, political theorists, and philosophers. Therefore, it is easier to deal with neoliberalism in its idealistic form than in the real world, due to its being "a messy hybrid from the start" (Peck, 2010, p. 39). Despite these drawbacks, neoliberalism has been used extensively to help understand what has happened to the state and society, including the education system. Marketisation in HE has been understood by many as, in essence, rooted in the neoliberal turn that has affected the whole planet. At face value, the drive for markets within all aspects of the social world would be a prime candidate for why and how marketisation occurred in HE. As such, neoliberalism must have been at work incorporating markets in HE.

This book has demonstrated that neoliberalism contains the explanation (*explanans*) of marketisation in HE as opposed to that which needs to be explained (*explanandum*), which would make marketisation part of neoliberalisation. Yet on its own, it is somewhat inadequate. Contemporary society is messy and complex in nature, and different perspectives, theories, and paradigms are needed to understand most social phenomena. For instance, various forces shape HE policy decisions, how actors respond to them, and how the sector interdependently changes over time, including those managing or designing HE.

This book has evaluated how useful the concept of neoliberalism is in explaining why and how marketisation has taken hold of the HE sector in England and elsewhere. Instead of making the data fit the concept, we can highlight where they are and how they can aid understanding. We can be more nuanced and precise and offer more agency to those who have accepted or worked towards greater competition and market forces. If neoliberalism is understood as the philosophy "dedicated to the extension of the market and market-like forms of governance, rule, and control across—tendentially at least—all spheres of social life" (Peck & Tickell, 2007, p. 28), we can clearly distinguish different dimensions or approaches of this philosophy.

Key Points

The key points from each chapter are as follows:

- Neoliberalism started to shape HE at a time when the aim of HE was increasingly seen as economic-instrumental framing (Chap. 2).
- Neoliberalism is fundamentally critical to government intervention if not in the service of the market (Chap. 3).
- Neoliberalism emphasises the value of markets and price systems, the meaninglessness of human subjectivity without ratification by the market, and that economic freedom is a condition of human freedom (Chap. 3).
- Neoliberalism has been applied to understand a wide range of processes and outcomes, either as policy, as ideology or as governmentality (Chap. 4).
- Neoliberalism as a concept is able to offer insights into understanding marketisation in a well-defined manner, but necessarily partially.

Contributions to Our Understanding of Marketisation

What does this mean for our understanding of marketisation? We have seen that the state plays a distinct role in HE's marketisation the English context. The aforementioned increase in state control of HE is possibly the most significant change in the governance of British HE, according to Shattock and Horvath (2019, pp. 153–154). This recent control exercised over HE moves beyond the introduction of markets and departs sharply from how neoliberalism constructs the state's responsibility. Also, the rationales behind increasing marketisation have been wide-ranging, often created ad hoc, and not always caused by a strong ideological drive. Competition between providers has been introduced to improve efficiency and offer students a greater choice of innovative and better-quality products and services. However, a real market has never taken off in the undergraduate provision. For instance, students cannot freely choose which course they want to access, there is no price mechanism for UG courses, and the student does not know how much they will repay.

The neoliberal commitment to laissez-faire regarding markets is based on the belief that they constitute a self-regulating order that produces knowledge and serves freedom in a way that planning never can. It regulates itself better than the government or any other outside force. In this, neoliberals demonstrate a distinct distrust of governmental power but are willing to use state power to further the reach and intensity of markets. The extension of state activity in all areas within HE is clearly not congruous with how a neoliberal state would act. A neoliberal state would naturally shy away from any intervention that does not promote the further reach of markets and the market mechanism. Recently, governments have taken away more autonomy from universities and have intervened in areas where they did not venture previously.

The transfer of responsibility that comes with marketisation is very much in line with a neoliberal position that is blind to market outcomes. The introduction of market competitions throughout HE shifts the focus to the allocation process (market) and moves away from ideas around fairness that would serve the interests of certain groups. Students need to take responsibility for the choices they make. Bad human capital investments result in suboptimal labour market outcomes, yet the market provides valuable information for others.

What Does This Mean for Our Understanding of Neoliberalisation?

One of the problems with neoliberalism is that there is no real consensus on what it means. However, most can agree that it is ultimately an active driver of social change driven by clear political and ideological motives. Davies (2014, p. 310) observed that definitions in the existing literature on neoliberalism tend to view it as "an inventive, constructivist, modernizing force" that foregrounds the notion of competition and aims to transform institutions that exist 'outside of the market' through the cooperation of the state. On that general level, the concept may work for the understanding of marketisation. However, even if we agree on the logic behind neoliberalism, there is no uniformity in how its practices are realised across different national, cultural, and local contexts. Therefore, we must look at the evidence of neoliberalism rather than assume that it has taken over the world or a section of it. As Peck et al. (2018, p. 4) argued:

> [N]eoliberalism plainly cannot exist in the world in 'pure', uncut, or unmediated form. Instead, its 'actually existing' manifestations are—and can only be—partial, polycentric, and plural [...] we have long made the case for processual understandings of neoliberalization, coupled with a recognition of the necessary diversity of its actually existing forms, the combined and uneven development of which is enduring but also mutually conditioning.

We can clearly see marketisation as an ongoing development, but it is not obvious what and what is not driven by neoliberalisation. How does neoliberalism reflect practice in HE? Fleming (2021, p. 8) asked the same question and observed a distinct exaggeration in how neoliberalism is played out:

> Are so-called 'neoliberal universities' truly neoliberal stricto sensu? The concept implies laissez-faire, minimal government intervention, privatization, competition and non-unionized workforces. However, most universities today only approximate this ideal, and are hardly the flexible, entrepreneurial corporate tigers so venerated by neoclassical economists.

The uneven evidence of neoliberalism as the major driver behind marketisation forces us to think about how particular approaches to neoliberalism can clarify certain parts of marketisation.

Neoliberalism as Policy

Policies that have driven further marketisation in the English context, such as the rise of undergraduate tuition fees in 2004 and 2012 or the removal of the cap on student numbers and the HE and Research Act (2017), cannot be understood solely through the lens of neoliberalism as policy. Some policies are indeed introduced to increase competition, which was thought to lead to increased responsiveness, flexibility, and rates of innovation. Informed choice is likewise thought to lead to improved quality of education and allocative efficiency. Yet the need for competition and the increase in tuition fees were driven by other rationales, including the need for greater access to HE and the need to reduce government spending, as well as a drive seemingly to align universities to the perceived demands of employers (Tholen, 2022). In other words, these policies are not always caused by a strong ideological drive. Governments have introduced pro-market policies using non-neoliberal political aims. From a policy perspective, neoliberal arguments are only one of the many initiatives driving policy. Policy rationales behind increasing marketisation have been wide-ranging and often created ad hoc. Here, public choice theory proponents may see examples of the state captured by special interests. Also, a real market has never taken off in the undergraduate provision.

While scholarly researchers may share some basic understandings of what a neoliberal HE system constitutes, it is far from a policy blueprint readily applicable anywhere. For McCaig (2018, p. 23), neoliberalism is "merely a framing device for often reactive policymaking"; in itself, "neoliberalism as a meta-discourse contributes relatively little to our understanding of the success or failure of marketisation arguments". The national context is crucial to understanding how much influence neoliberal ideas have on policy. McCaig et al. (2018) argued that neoliberalism is contingent and variable and will shape itself to co-exist with other policy drivers depending on these national contexts. The authors observed:

> All governments have to reconcile competition, marketisation, and equality in HE and appear to attempt to achieve this by distancing themselves from the need to take remedial action and by re-framing 'equality' as 'equity' and 'fairness'—terms which are better attuned to economistic and national competitiveness agenda's (McCaig et al., 2018, p. 20)

Neoliberalism as a policy shifts responsibility for the welfare of its citizens to the individual (through an active but highly focused state). Marketisation in HE certainly does this, but at the same time, the UK government has intervened so much in the HE market and set numerous conditions and barriers, creating a highly regulated marketplace instead of anything resembling a free or capitalist market.

Neoliberalism as Ideology

The second approach understands neoliberalism as a form of ideology that goes far beyond the policy domain. As Gane (2012, pp. 629–630) noted, "neoliberalism is not simply about deregulation, privatization, or governing through freedom, but also about intervention and regulation with the aim of injecting market principles of competition into all forms of social and cultural life". Whether neoliberalism, understood as a capitalist ideology, drives marketisation in HE is difficult to say. We can see how ideas around the notion of HE as an investment good would relieve the state from some responsibility for citizens' economic opportunities.

Some argue that marketisation demonstrates the university's role in contributing to the economic productivity of the country, serving capitalist interest in skill formation (e.g. Mioasuria & Cole, 2017). It is true that marketisation policies explicitly mention the interests of employers and their skill needs, which they align with the interests of students (Tholen, 2022), yet it is rather unclear what impact marketisation has on productivity.

The idea of consumer sovereignty is instilled in marketisation and can be seen as part of a neoliberal ideology. According to neoliberals, consumers exercise their freedom through the choices they make in the marketplace. Their power is expressed in their role as market actors. Thus, Mises (1944, p. 227) argued that:

> [t]he real bosses are the consumers. They, by their buying and by their abstention from buying, decide who should own the capital and run the plants. They determine what should be produced and in what quantity and quality. Their attitudes result either in profit or in loss for the enterprise. They make poor men rich and rich men poor.

Student consumerism may also be seen as something that has slowly crept into the system by design or otherwise, but it was not part of HE for centuries (Hussey & Smith, 2010; Williams, 2013). Understanding students' identity and status and the relationship between them and their institution as a market exchange is ultimately largely ideological. A way of thinking about the world underpins the students as a consumer perspective and obscures other views on what HE can or should accomplish. In neoliberalism (and perhaps clearest in ordoliberalism), market principles can be applied to everything, and in all areas of life, the market and its principles are simply everywhere. This worldview has become more grounded in practice in everyday HE but whether this perspective is dominant should be questioned or challenged. Ultimately, neoliberalism as an ideology is about privileging forms of knowledge and creating a lens through which all aspects of life are understood. Are people seeing their education purely in market terms? Given the fierce battles in the public domain over what HE should be, the consumerist perspective is not entirely hegemonic. However, we can also see forms of acceptance in the views and behaviour of both students and academics.

The Marxist insistence that ideology represents the interest of capital or capitalism can be seen in how modern universities behave and are organised. Forms of value extraction and exploitation are, for instance, manifest in how universities manage their workers and the commercialisation of knowledge production through research links with industry (Moore et al., 2021). Also, public universities have become increasingly subsumed in a global education market in which so-called academic capitalist forces drive the institutions' activities, missions, and incentives (Börjesson & Dalberg, 2021; Kauppinen, 2012; Marginson, 2007). There are many other areas where neoliberalism as an ideology cannot capture how, in practice, markets are applied within HE systems.

Neoliberalisation as Governmentality

The third and final approach is neoliberalism as governmentality, which serves as a valuable perspective for understanding marketisation. It asserts that neoliberalism is everywhere and expresses itself as practices of everyday life, including our language, purposes, decisions, and social relations (Ball & Olmedo, 2013, p. 88). The neoliberal subject is a moral subject in specific ways. Neoliberalism as governmentality captures how social and personal life in its entirety is remade around an ideal of enterprise and performance. The ethos of competitiveness permeates not just the government but also culture, education, and personal relations and orientation to the self. Dardot and Laval (2013, p. 261) noted:

> Neo-liberal rationality produces the subject it requires by deploying the means of governing himself so that he really does conduct himself as an entity in competition, who must maximise his results by exposing himself to risks and taking responsibility for possible failures. 'Enterprise' is thus the name to be given to self-government in the neo-liberal age.

There exists an individual obligation to adopt a prudent and market-oriented relationship to risk and to life more generally (Du Gay, 1996, p. 2000). Although students do not necessarily accept the role of consumer, the way marketisation has positioned them makes governmentality helpful in understanding the self-governance that takes place in students. With greater private investment in the English context came great responsibility. O'Malley (1992) understands responsibilisation as a key governmental practice creating self-interested market subjects who are forced to make choices about their lifestyles, education, health, and welfare without relying on the state.

Likewise, neoliberal governmentality creates subjects working within HE. With marketisation came an increased emphasis on performance and accountability assessment, accompanied by performance indicators and appraisal. Gane (2012, p. 629) defined the "active processes of (self-) government and (self-) surveillance that come from the market and which, most commonly, take the form of audit". Neoliberalism has thus advocated a shift in the forms of accountability akin to the market, using quantifiable output measures and market conceptualisation of what constitutes success and failure. As Ball (2017, p. 217) reminds us,

> This is a system of education that at each level, from the national to the student, is modelled on the firm, an investment model that requires students, teachers and schools to make decisions about how they invest their time, resources and energy in relation to likely returns—as qualifications and labour market opportunities, as performance improvement, as social advantage. Individuals and families must take responsibility for their own performance and their own improvement.

As we have seen in the previous chapters, we can point to specific instances and situations in which participants in HE are asked to become competitive, instrumentally rational subjects who can compete in the marketplace.

A NEW APPROACH: NEOLIBERALISATION AS A WIDER SHIFT

There is no one version of neoliberalism that can understand marketisation on its own, nor do the three perspectives individually offer a satisfactory framework. How can we think about neoliberalism in a way that can elucidate its impact on marketisation? Chapter 2 outlined a change in how universities and their purposes are viewed. Over time, distinct economic-instrumental aims have been set both externally and internally by HE institutions. They pointed at how HE could help drive economic growth through human capital formation and technological progress, as well as an engine of social mobility. These purposes have grown and overshadowed the other roles HE used to take within public discourses and policy circles.

The dominance of an economic-instrumental view of HE should be seen as a crucial condition under which marketisation occurs. This view treats HE as a means to an end that allows individuals and the state to benefit economically from HE participation. Existing ideas on the role of HE and how universities should be structured can help us to understand why neoliberalism has held sway. Tomicic (2019) saw a dichotomy between the goals of universities inspired by the ideals of Humboldt and Newman and those informed by the pursuit of (market-driven) neoliberalism. According to Tomicic, university policymakers are presented with two conflicting visions to choose from: Humboldtian idealism or neoliberal utilitarianism (p. 1060). The author is pessimistic, as the university concept has "not only been transformed from its original ideals, but also has critically damaged its own potential future" (Tomicic, 2019, p. 1058).

However, it is important not to *equate* the economic-instrumental view with neoliberalism. Neoliberalism is a more specific position on the role of the market and, at the same time, encompasses many more political ideas, including on the role of the state. Ultimately, we need to treat the intrinsic non-economic and economic-instrumental views of HE as ideal types. As shown in Chap. 2, there has always been an economic-instrumental dimension to our understanding of HE. For most of their existence, universities were independent private, autonomous, and nonprofit institutions that operated with limited government policies or regulations. It is important to note that the loss of autonomy of universities started much earlier than in the 1980s. After 1949, when it increased its financial support, the UK government exerted significant influence on how universities were governed, student participation rates, and what was taught and researched within HE (Shattock, 2013). Similarly, capitalism (in particular, in the US context) has been shaping HE long before neoliberalism. As Saunders (2010, 55) argued,

> The changes that have occurred due to neoliberalism are not fundamental transformations of the roles and purposes of the university, but instead are substantial accentuations of its previous functions. To say that the development of the neoliberal university and the changes that define it are unique is to both misunderstand the history of HE in the United States as well as to misplace the source of many functions of HE. What is new to the neoliberal university is the scope and extent of these profit-driven, corporate ends, as well as how many students, faculty, administrators, and policy makers explicitly support and embrace these capitalistic goals and priorities.

However, what is argued here is that the economic instrument view made neoliberal influence less difficult to achieve and more profound in its power. Neoliberalism is strengthened by the economic-instrumental view while simultaneously contributing to it. Neoliberalism has become one of several forces shaping HE today, instead of a hegemonic behemoth taking on the public sector and universities. Even in England, where arguably, the influence of neoliberalism is more clearly observed than in other European countries, it is never more than partial and contingent. On the policy level, economic market reform is only one policy agenda within the HE sector. On the ideological level, the market is not the only producer of cultural logic and value (Lynch, 2006). On the subjective level, other discourses that resist or are incompatible with neoliberal government are present and also make up the subject.

This imperfect application of the concept of neoliberalism may reflect the true nature of neoliberalisation, which does not come in a pure form. Neoliberalism, once in power, finds out that its theory of market and competition leads to unexpected, undesirable outcomes, and so it adapts itself. As Peck (2010, p. 13) suggests, neoliberalism is

> a self-contradictory form of regulation-in-denial. It does not glide forward along some teleological track, it tends to lurch three steps forward and two steps back, in the form of an adaptive mutating, and contradictory mode of governance.

Another way we can place the role of neoliberalism within a wider economic utilitarianism is if we see neoliberalism as a force of economisation, the dominance of economics in understanding society and the social, applying the economic logic to all areas of life, including those traditionally not part of it. William Davies (2017) interpreted neoliberalism as economics pursuing politics. Davies developed the idea that what sets neoliberalism apart is its insistence that "economics should be a better analytical basis for government than other political or scientific forms of authority" (Davies, 2017, p. 10). HE is part of a market. In other words, where neoliberalism fits best is taken "as market-based (or market-derived) forms of economization, calculation, measurement and valuations" (Davies, 2017, p. 22), in other words, the spirit of competitiveness that has permeated HE. Given that markets in education are so far removed from a free market, neoliberalist insistence that the market will produce optimal outcomes if the price mechanism can connect supply and demand unhindered by the state is not the key insight that helps understand how neoliberalism is applied in HE. What we call marketisation is not so much the advancement of markets but more about the expanding reach of market-based principles and techniques of evaluation markets (Davies, 2017, p. 23).

Conclusion

Whether neoliberalism is 'responsible' for marketisation in HE may, at first sight, not make a great deal of difference to those experiencing it. Students, academics, university administrators, and policymakers will recognise marketisation, whether caused by neoliberalism or not. Yet, politically, a pushback to marketisation often relies on a rejection of neoliberalism. The United States is an extreme case. The financing of American HE has shifted radically towards the user, with a decline in government contribution (Newfield, 2018; Corrigan, 2023). Increased tuition fees come with larger individual student debts (Honderich, 2022). The student loan debt balance in the United States has increased by 66% over the past decade, totalling more than $1.77 trillion in 2023 (Chernikoff, 2023). With many graduates struggling to repay their student loans, combined with stark ethnic, gender, and class inequalities in individual debt, these issues are part of broader political debates about opportunity and inter-generational social mobility. Student loans are less of a political issue in the UK, but many graduates feel their impact. Graduates in England currently leave university with average debts of £44,940 (Jones, 2024), and some graduates express emotional and psychological distress because of their large student debts (Busby, 2021).

Worldwide, academics protest against the deteriorating working conditions associated with marketisation. It is important to note that countries that have resisted marketisation are by no means free of trouble. Underfunding has also led to pressure on universities and academics. Also, caps on the number of university places have driven increased competition between school leavers, which often leads to class-based inequalities in participation (e.g. Isopahkala-Bouret, 2019).

Despite marketisation now being a reality in many countries, it still matters to what extent it is driven by neoliberalism. It is significant for those who want to understand how we got here and why marketised systems, such as the English one, are so different from other Western countries. For those wishing to stop or turn back marketisation, it is essential to know what drives marketisation. If we understand neoliberalism as a policy, we may want to pressure governments to change policies. If we understand neoliberalism as an ideology, we may be up against larger capitalist forces responsible for HE changes that reflect the interests of capital and capitalism. If neoliberalism is understood as governmentality, it could actively unpack and resist discourses that contribute to people thinking of themselves as market actors instead of citizens of the public domain.

Equally important is the realisation that more than neoliberal forces are at play. It may be more helpful to think about the dominance of an economic-instrumental view of HE as a crucial condition under which marketisation has occurred and is supported by neoliberalism. Over time, HE policies were actively endorsed by ideas on the role of human capital in economic growth, technological progress, and social mobility. Over time, these purposes have grown and overshadowed other purposes within public discourses and policy circles. The use of markets to run HE is more than a solution to a distinct problem such as the growing crisis of affordability. We are not powerless to shape HE. The formation of the modern university does not start with the emergence of neoliberalism. It changes all the time and is far from fixed. Likewise, our thinking about what HE should do is far from set in stone. It would be a mistake to assume that the apparent persistence of neoliberalism is inevitable and everlasting.

REFERENCES

Ball, S. J. (2017). *The Education Debate – Policy and Politics in the Twenty-First Century* (3rd ed.). Bristol University Press.

Ball, S. J., & Olmedo, A. (2013). Care of the self, resistance and subjectivity under neoliberal, governmentalities. *Critical Studies in Education, 54*(1), 85–96.

Börjesson, M., & Dalberg, T. (2021). Massification, unification, marketisation, internationalisation: A socio-political history of higher education in Sweden 1945–2020. *European Journal of Higher Education, 11*(3), 346–364.

Busby, E. (2021). Graduates experience 'psychological disturbance' over student loan debt – report. *The Standard*, November 26. Retrieved April 24, 2024, from https://www.standard.co.uk/news/uk/graduates-student-loans-company-government-england-english-b968145.html

Chernikoff, S. (2023). Student loan repayments: These charts explain how much student debt Americans owe. *USA Today*, October 3. Retrieved April 24, 2024, from https://eu.usatoday.com/story/money/2023/10/03/student-loan-repayments-charts-show-debt-crisis/71035530007/

Corrigan, L. M. (2023). The evisceration of a public university. *The Nation*, August 16. Retrieved April 24, 2024, from https://www.thenation.com/article/society/wvu-cuts-higher-education/

Dardot, P., & Laval, C. (2013). *The New Way of the World: On Neoliberal Society*. Verso books.

Davies, W. (2014). Neoliberalism: A bibliographic review. *Theory, Culture & Society, 31*(7–8), 309–317.

Davies, W. 2017. *The limits of neoliberalism: Authority, sovereignty, and the logic of competition* (Revised ed.). Sage.

Du Gay, P. (1996). *Consumption and identity at work*. Sage.

Fleming, P. (2021). The ghost university: Academe from the ruins. *Emancipations: A Journal of Critical Social Analysis, 1*(1) Article 4.

Gane, N. (2012). The governmentalities of neoliberalism: Panopticism, post-panopticism and beyond. *The Sociological Review, 60*(4), 611–634.

Honderich, H. (2022). Student loan forgiveness: Biden cancels $10,000 in student debt for millions. *BBC News*, August 24. Retrieved April 24, 2024, from https://www.bbc.co.uk/news/world-us-canada-62664181

Hussey, T., & Smith, P. (2010). *The Trouble with Higher Education*. Routledge.

Isopahkala-Bouret, U. (2019). Troublesome access. Non-admission experiences in a competitive finnish higher education. *Social Sciences, 8*(11), 302.

Jones, H. (2024). Student loans: UK's highest debt revealed to be £231,000. *BBC News*, March 22. Retrieved April 24, 2024, from https://www.bbc.co.uk/news/uk-68534953

Kauppinen, I. (2012). Towards transnational academic capitalism. *Higher Education, 64*(4), 543–556.

Lynch, K. (2006). Neo-liberalism and marketisation: The implications for higher education. *European Educational Research Journal, 5*(1), 1–17.

Maisuria, A., & Cole, M. (2017). The neoliberalization of higher education in England: An alternative is possible. *Policy Futures in Education, 15*(5), 602–619.

Marginson, S. (2007). The public/private division in higher education: A global revision. *Higher Education, 53*(3), 307–333.

McCaig, C. (2018). *The Marketisation of English Higher Education: A Policy Analysis of a Risk-Based System*. Emerald.

McCaig, C., M. Bowl, & J. Hughes, J. (2018). Conceptualising equality, equity and differentiation in marketised higher education: Fractures and fault-lines in the neoliberal imaginary. In: M. Bowl, C. McCaig, and Hughes, J. (Eds.), *Equality and Differentiation in Marketised Higher Education: A New Level Playing Field?* (pp. 195–220). Palgrave.

Michie, J. (2019). *The Handbook of Globalisation* (3rd ed.). Edward Elgar.

Mises, L. (1944). *Bureaucracy*. Yale University Press.

Moore, R. (2021). The free-market gamble: Has Covid broken UK universities? *The Guardian*, January 17. Retrieved April 24, 2024, from https://www.theguardian.com/education/2021/jan/17/free-market-gamble-has-covid-broken-uk-universities

Newfield, C. (2018). *The Great Mistake: How We Wrecked Public Universities and How We Can Fix Them*. Johns Hopkins University Press.

O'Malley, P. (1992). Risk, power and crime prevention. *Economy & Society*, *21*(3), 252–275.

Peck, J. (2010). *Constructions of Neoliberal Reason*. Oxford University Press.

Peck, J., Brenner, N., Theodore, N., & N. (2018). Actually existing neoliberalism. In D. Cahill, M. Cooper, M. Konings, & D. Primrose (Eds.), *The Sage Handbook of Neoliberalism* (pp. 3–15). Sage.

Peck, J., & Tickell, A. (2007). Conceptualizing neoliberalism, thinking Thatcherism. In H. Leitner, J. Peck, & E. S. Sheppard (Eds.), *Contesting Neoliberalism: Urban Frontie* (pp. 26–50). Guilford Press.

Saunders, D. B. (2010). Neoliberal ideology and public higher education in the United States. *Journal for Critical Education Policy Studies*, *8*(1), 41–77. 201.

Shattock, M. (2013). University governance, leadership and management in a decade of diversification and uncertainty. *Higher Education Quarterly*, *67*(3), 217–233.

Shattock, M., & Horvath, A. (2019). *The governance of british higher education the impact of governmental, financial and market pressures*. Bloomsbury.

Tholen, G. (2022). *Modern Work and the Marketisation of Higher Education*. Policy Press.

Tomicic, A. (2019). American dream, Humboldtian nightmare: Reflections on the remodelled values of a neoliberalized academia. *Policy Futures in Education*, *17*(8), 1057–1077.

Williams, J. (2013). *Consuming Higher Education: Why Learning Can't Be Bought*. Bloomsbury.

References

Abercrombie, N., & Turner, B. (1978). The dominant ideology thesis. *British Journal of Sociology, 29*(2), 149–170.

Adam, R., & Weale, S. (2022). Ministers' loan plans could stop poorer students in England going to university. *The Guardian*, February 22. Retrieved April 24, 2024, from https://www.theguardian.com/education/2022/feb/22/fears-that-minimum-grades-for-student-loans-in-england-could-narrow-access

Adams, R. (2020a). Ministers to ditch target of 50% of young people in England going to university *The Guardian*, July 9. Retrieved April 24, 2024, from https://www.theguardian.com/politics/2020/jul/09/ministers-to-ditch-target-of-50-of-young-people-in-england-going-to-university

Adams, R. (2020b). Minister lambasts English universities for letting down students. *The Guardian*, July 1. Retrieved April 24, 2024, from https://www.theguardian.com/education/2020/jul/01/minister-lambasts-uk-universities-policy-for-letting-down-students

Adams, R. (2022a). Students show 'shocking growth in support for censorship', ministers warn. *The Guardian*, June 23. Retrieved April 24, 2024, from https://www.theguardian.com/education/2022/jun/23/students-shocking-growth-support-censorship-ministers-warn

Adams, R. (2022b). England and Wales university fees 'bad value for money' – survey. *The Guardian*, August 31. https://www.theguardian.com/education/2022/aug/31/england-and-wales-university-feesbad-value-for-money-survey

Agasisti, T., & Catalano, G. (2006). Governance models of university systems – towards quasi-markets? Tendencies and perspectives: A European comparison. *Journal of Higher Education Policy and Management, 28*(3), 245–262.

Amable, B. (2011). Morals and politics in the ideology of neo-liberalism. *Socio-Economic Review, 9*(1), 3–30.

Anderson, R. (2006). *British Universities Past and Present*. Bloomsbury.

Anderson, R. (2010). The 'idea of a university' today. History and policy. Policy papers. Retrieved April 22, 2024, from https://www.historyandpolicy.org/policy-papers/papers/the-idea-of-a-university-today

Apple, M. (2000). *Ideology and Curriculum*. Routledge Falmer.

Aranowitz, S. (2001a). *The Knowledge Factory: Dismantling the Corporate University and Creating True Higher Learning*. Beacon Press.

Archer, L. (2008). The new neoliberal subjects? Young/er academics' constructions of professional identity. *Journal of Education Policy, 23*(3), 265–285.

Ashwin, P. (2020). *Transforming University Education: A Manifesto*. Bloomsbury.

Association of Colleges. (2020). *The Impact of Competition in Post-16 Education & Training*. AoC.

Balan, A. (2023). Neoliberalism, privatisation and marketisation: The implications for legal education in England and Wales. *Cogent Education, 10*(2).

Ball, S. (2012). Performativity, commodification, and commitment: An I-Spy guide to the neoliberal university. *British Journal of Educational Studies, 60*(1), 17–28.

Ball, S. (2017). *The Education Debate – Policy and Politics in the Twenty-First Century* (3rd ed.). Bristol University Press.

Ball, S. J. (2003). The teacher's soul and the terrors of performativity. *Journal of Education Policy, 18*(2), 215–228.

Ball, S. J. (2015). Living the neo-liberal University. *European Journal of Education, 50*(3), 258–261.

Baltodano, M.P. 2014. Neoliberalism and the demise of public education: The corporatization of schools of education. In: *The Globalization and Corporatization of Education: Limits and Liminality of the Market Mantra*, eds. D. Blum D. and C. Ullman, 121–141. : Routledge.

Barkan, J. (2018). Corporate power and neoliberalism. In D. Cahill, M. Cooper, M. Konings, & D. Primrose (Eds.), *The Sage Handbook of Neoliberalism* (pp. 446–456). Sage.

Barnett, C. (2009). Publics and Markets: What's Wrong with Neoliberalism? In S. Smith, R. Pain, S. Marston, & J. P. Jones (Eds.), *The Sage Handbook of Social Geography* (pp. 269–296). Sage.

Barnett, R. (2000). *Realising the University in an Age of Supercomplexity*. Open University Press.

Becker, G. S. (1964). *Human Capital: A Theoretical and Empirical Analysis, with Special Reference to Education*. Chicago University Press.

Becker, G. S. (1990). *The Economic Approach to Human Behavior*. Chicago University Press.
Becker, G. S. (1993). The economic way of looking at behavior. *Journal of Political Economy, 101*(3), 385–409.
Behrent, M. (2009). Liberalism without humanism: Michel Foucault and the free market creed 1976–1979. *Modern Intellectual History, 6*(3), 539–568.
Biebrichter, T. (2018). *The Political Theory of Neoliberalism*. Stanford University Press.
Birch, K. (2015a). Neoliberalism: The whys and wherefores ... and future directions. *Sociology Compass, 9*(7), 571–584.
Birch, K. (2015b). *We Have Never Been Neoliberal*. Zero Books.
Birch, K. (2017). *A Research Agenda for Neoliberalism*. Edward Elgar.
Blackmore, P., & Kandiko, C. B. (2011). Motivation in academic life: A prestige economy. *Research in Post-Compulsory Education, 16*(4), 399–411.
Blaug, M. (1976). The empirical status of human capital theory: A slightly jaundiced survey. *Journal of Economic Literature, 14*(3), 827–855.
Block, F., & Somers, M. R. (2014). *The Power of Market Fundamentalism: Karl Polanyi's Critique*. Harvard University.
Blyth, M. (2002). *Great Transformations: Economic Ideas and Institutional Change in the Twentieth Century*. Cambridge University Press.
Boas, T. C., & Gans-Morse, J. (2009). Neoliberalism: From new liberal philosophy to anti-liberal slogan. *Studies in Comparative International Development, 44*(2), 137–161.
Boden, R., & Epstein, D. (2006). Managing the research imagination? Globalisation and research in higher education. *Globalisation, Societies and Education, 4*(2), 223–236.
Bok, D. (2003). *Universities in the Marketplace: The Commercialization of Higher Education*. Princeton University Press.
Bolton, P. (2024). *Research Briefing House of Commons Library*. Higher Education student numbers, 2 January. Retrieved April 24, 2024, from https://commonslibrary.parliament.uk/research-briefings/cbp-7857/
Bowl, M. (2018). Diversity and differentiation, equity and equality in a marketised higher education system. In M. Bowl, C. McCaig, & J. Hughes (Eds.), *Equality and Differentiation in Marketised Higher Education. Palgrave Studies in Excellence and Equity in Global Education* (pp. 1–20). Palgrave Macmillan.
Bradley, S., Draca, M., & Green, C. (2004). School performance in Australia: Is there a role for quasimarkets? *Australian Economic Review, 37*(3), 271–286.
Bragg, S. (2007). Student voice and governmentality: The production of enterprising subject. *Discourse: Studies in the Cultural Politics of Education, 28*(3), 343–355.
Brazzill, M. (2021). The development of higher education in Japan and the United Kingdom: The impact of neoliberalism. *Higher Education Quarterly, 75*(3), 381–397.

Brenner, N., & Theodore, N. (Eds.). (2002). *Spaces of Neoliberalism: Urban Restructuring in North America and Western Europe*. Blackwell.

Britton, J., L. Dearden, L., L. van der Erve, and B. Waltmann. 2020. The Impact of Undergraduate Degrees on Lifetime Earnings. : IFS.

Briziarelli, M. and J.L. Flores, J. L 2018. Professing contradictions: Knowledge work and the-neoliberal condition of academic workers. *tripleC Communication, Capitalism and Critique* 16 (1): 114–128.

Brooks, R., Byford, K., & Sela, K. (2016a). Students' unions, consumerism and the neo-liberal university. *British Journal of Sociology of Education, 37*(8), 1–19.

Brooks, R., Byford, K., & Sela, K. (2016b). Students' unions, consumerism and the neo-liberal university. *British Journal of Sociology of Education, 37*(8), 1211–1228.

Brown, P and H. Lauder, H. 2001. *Capitalism and Social Progress: The Future of Society in a Global Economy*. : Palgrave.

Brown, P., Lauder, H., Ashton, D., Yingje, W., & Vincent-Lancrin, S. (2008). Education, globalisation and the future of the knowledge economy. *European Educational Research Journal, 7*(2), 131–156.

Brown, P., H. Lauder, H. and S.Y. Cheung. 2020. *The Death of Human Capital: Its Failed Promise and How to Renew it*. : Oxford University Press.

Brown, R. (Ed.). (2011a). *Higher Education and the Market*. Routledge.

Brown, R. (2011b). Introduction. In R. Brown (Ed.), *Higher Education and the Market* (pp. 1–6). Routledge.

Brown, R. (2011c). The impact of markets. In R. Brown (Ed.), *Higher Education and the Market* (pp. 20–52). Routledge.

Brown, R. (2013). *Everything for Sale? The Marketization of UK Higher Education*. Routledge.

Brown, R. (2018). *Neoliberalism, Marketisation and Higher Education*. Speech Edge Hill University, June 14. Retrieved April 22, 2024, from https://www.youtube.com/watch?v=pMpiiVxNd8g

Brown, R. & P. Scott. (2009). *The Role of the Market in Higher Education*. Retrieved April 24, 2024, from https://www.hepi.ac.uk/2009/03/18/the-role-of-the-market-in-higher-education/

Brown, W. (2011d). Neoliberalized knowledge. *History of the Present, 1*(1), 113–129.

Brown, W. (2015). *Undoing the Demos: Neoliberalism's Stealth Revolution*. Zone Books.

Buchanan, J., Wagner, M., Richard, E., & Burton, J. (1978). *The Consequences of Mr. Keynes*. London.

Buchanan, J. M. (1975). *The Limits of Liberty: Between Anarchy and Leviathan*. Chicago University of Chicago Press.

Buchanan, J. M. (1986). *Liberty, Market and State*. New York University Press.

Bunce, L., Baird, A., & Jones, S. E. (2017). The student as consumer approach in higher education and its effects on academic performance. *Studies in Higher Education*, 2(11), 1958–1978.

Burchell, G. (1996). Liberal government and techniques of the self. In A. Barry, T. Osborne, & N. Rose (Eds.), *Foucault and Political Reason* (pp. 19–36). University of Chicago Press.

Burgin, A. (2012). *The Great Persuasion: Reinventing Free Markets since the Depression*. Harvard University Press.

Burton, S., & Bowman, B. (2022). The academic precariat: Understanding life and labour in the neoliberal academy. *British Journal of Sociology of Education*, 43(4), 497–512.

Busby, E. (2018). Minister criticises universities so overcrowded students 'forced to stand at back of lecture halls without desk'. *The Independent*, June 7. Retrieved April 24, 2024, from https://www.independent.co.uk/news/education/education-news/students-universities-sam-gyimah-vice-chancellors-tuition-fees-graduate-earnings-lecture-halls-a8387701.html

Caldwell, B. (2004). *Hayek's Challenge: An Intellectual Biography of F.A. Hayek*. University of Chicago Press.

Callon, M. (2021). *Markets in the Making: Rethinking Competition, Goods, and Innovation*. Zone Books.

Cannizzo, F. (2015). Academic subjectivities: Governmentality and self-development in higher education. *Foucault Studies*, 20, 199–217.

Carasso, H., & Locke, W. (2015). Paying the price of expansion: Why more for undergraduates in England means less for everyone. In P. John & J. Fanghanel (Eds.), *Dimensions of Marketisation in Higher Education* (pp. 26–37). Routledge.

Carpentier, V. (2015). The historical expansion of higher education in Europe: Spaces, shapes and rationales. In J. L. Rury & E. H. Tamura (Eds.), *The Oxford Handbook of The History of Education* (pp. 259–274). Oxford University Press.

Carpentier, V. (2018). Expansion and differentiation in higher education: The historical trajectories of the UK, the USA and France. In *CGHE Working Paper 33*. Centre for Global Higher Education.

Carpentier, V. (2019). Higher education in modern Europe. In J. L. Rury & E. H. Tamura (Eds.), *The Oxford Handbook of the History of Education* (pp. 259–274). Oxford University Press.

Chang, H.-J. (2002). Breaking the mould: An institutionalist political economy alternative to the neo-liberal theory of the market and the state. *Cambridge Journal of Economics*, 26(5), 539–559.

Chomsky, N. (1998). *Profit Over People: Neoliberalism and Global Order*. Seven Stories Press.

Clark, W. (2006). *Academic Charisma and the Origins of the Research University*. University of Chicago Press.

Clarke, J., Newman, J., & Westmarland, L. (2007). The antagonisms of choice: New labour and the reform of public services. *Social Policy & Society*, 7(2), 245–253.
Clegg, S.R., D. Courpasson, D., and N. Phillips. 2006. *Power and Organizations*. : Sage
Coates, K. (2016). Playing to the numbers. *Prometheus*, 34(1), 73–77.
Collini, S. (2012). *What Are Universities For?* Penguin.
Collini, S. (2013). Sold out. *London Review of Books*, 35(20), 3–12.
Collini, S. (2017). *Speaking of Universities*. Verso Books.
Connell, R. (2013). The neoliberal cascade and education: An essay on the market agenda and its consequences. *Critical Studies in Education*, 54(2), 99–112.
Cooper, M. (2020). Neoliberalism's family values: Welfare, human capital, and kinship. In P. Mirowski, D. Plehwe, & Q. Slobodian (Eds.), *Nine Lives of Neoliberalism* (pp. 95–119). Verso Books.
Couldry, N. (2011). Fighting for the university's life. In M. Bailey & D. Freedman (Eds.), *The Assault on Universities: A Manifesto for Resistance* (pp. 37–48). Pluto.
Craig, D., & Cotterell, G. (2007). Periodising neoliberalism? *Policy & Politics*, 35(3), 497–514.
Crouch, C. (2011). *The Strange Non-Death of Neoliberalism*. Polity Press.
Daniels, R.J. with G. Shreve and P. Spector 2021. *What Universities Owe Democracy*. : John Hopkins University Press.
Dardot, P., & Laval, C. (2013). *The New Way of the World: On Neoliberal Society*. Verso books.
Das, S. (2023). UK universities paying millions in agent fees to secure international students. *The Guardian*, November 18. Retrieved April 24, 2024, from https://www.theguardian.com/education/2023/nov/18/uk-universities-paying-millions-in-agent-fees-to-secure-international-students
Davies, B. (2005). The (im)possibility of intellectual work in neoliberal regimes. *Discourse: Studies in the Cultural Politics of Education*, 26(1), 1–14.
Davies, B., & Bansel, P. (2007). Neoliberalism and education. *International Journal of Qualitative Studies in Education*, 20(3), 247–259.
Davies, B., & Bansel, P. (2010). Governmentality and academic work: Shaping the hearts and minds of academic workers. *Journal of Curriculum Theorizing*, 26(3), 5–20.
Davies, B., Gottsche, M., & Bansel, P. (2006). The rise and fall of the neo-liberal university. *European Journal of Education*, 41(2), 305–319.
Davies, W., & Gane, N. (2021). Post-neoliberalism? An introduction. *Theory, Culture & Society*, 38(6), 3–28.
De La Fuente, J. R. (2002). Academic freedom and social responsibility. *Higher Education Policy*, 15(4), 337–339.
de Ridder-Symoens, H. (1992). *A History of the University in Europe. Vol. I. Universities in the Middle Ages*. Cambridge University Press.

Dean, M. (1995). Governing the unemployed self in an active society. *Economy and Society, 24*(4), 559–583.
Dean, M. (1999). *Governmentality: Power and Rule in Modern Society*. Sage.
Dean, M. (2007). *Governing Societies: Political Perspectives on Domestic and International Rule*. Open University Press.
Dean, M. (2014). Rethinking neoliberalism. *Journal of Sociology, 50*(2), 150–163.
Dean, M. (2018). Foucault and the neoliberalism controversy. In D. Cahill, M. Cooper, M. Konings, & D. Primrose (Eds.), *The Sage Handbook of Neoliberalism* (pp. 40–53). Sage.
Dearing, R. (1997). *Higher Education in the Learning Society*. HMSO.
Deem, R. (2001). Globalisation, new managerialism, academic capitalism and entrepreneurialism in universities: Is the local dimension still important? *Comparative Education, 37*(1), 7–20.
Deem, R., & Brehony, K. J. (2005). Management as ideology: The case of "new managerialism" in higher education. *Oxford Review of Education, 31*(2), 217–235.
Deem, R., Hillyard, S., & Reed, M. I. (2007). *Knowledge, Higher Education, and the New Managerialism: The Changing Management of UK Universities*. Oxford University Press.
Del Cerro Santamaría, G. D. (2020). Challenges and drawbacks in the marketisation of higher education within neoliberalism. *Review of European Studies, 12*(1), 22–38.
Department for Business, Innovation and Skills. (2015). *Fulfilling our Potential: Teaching Excellence, Social Mobility and Student Choice*. HM Government.
Department for Business, Innovation and Skills (DBIS). (2009). *Higher Ambitions: The Future of Universities in a Knowledge Economy*. London.
Department for Business, Innovation and Skills (DBIS). (2011). *Students at the Heart of the System*. London.
Department for Business Innovation and Skills (DBIS). (2016). *Success as a Knowledge Economy: Teaching Excellence, Social Mobility and Student Choice*. HM Government.
Department for Education (DfE). (2023a). Crackdown on rip-off university degrees. Retrieved April 24, 2024, from https://www.gov.uk/government/news/crackdown-on-rip-off-university-degrees
Department for Education (DfE). (2023b). University freedom of speech bill becomes law. Retrieved April 24, 2024, from https://www.gov.uk/government/news/university-freedom-of-speech-bill-becomes-law
DES. (1991). *Education and Training for the Twenty-first Century* (Vol. 2 vols). HMSO.
Dill, D. D. (1997). Higher education markets and public policy. *Higher Education Policy, 10*(3), 167–185.

Dill, D. D. (2003). Allowing the market to rule: The case of the United States. *Higher Education Quarterly, 57*(2), 136–157.
Dill, D. D., & Soo, M. (2005). Academic quality, league tables, and public policy: A cross-national analysis of university ranking systems. *Higher Education, 49*(4), 495–533.
Doherty, R. A. (2007). Education, neoliberalism and the consumer citizen: After the golden age of egalitarian reform. *Critical Studies in Education, 48*(2), 269–288.
Dougherty, K. J., & Natow, R. S. (2020). Performance-based funding for higher education: How well does neoliberal theory capture neoliberal practice? *Higher Education, 80*(3), 457–478.
Driver, S., & Martell, L. (2006). *New Labour* (2nd ed.). Polity Press.
Duménil, G., & Lévy, D. (2004). *Capital Resurgent: Roots of the Neoliberal Revolution.* Harvard University Press.
Duménil, G., & Levy, D. (2011). *The Crisis of Neoliberalism.* Harvard University Press.
Duménil, G., Lévy, D., & D. (2005). The neoliberal (counter-) revolution. In A. Saad-Filho & D. Johnston (Eds.), *Neoliberalism: A Critical Reader* (pp. 9–19). Pluto Press.
Duncan, G. (2024). Rishi Sunak summons university leaders after warning UK is descending into 'mob rule. *The National News.* February 29. Retrieved April 24, 2024, from https://www.thenationalnews.com/world/uk-news/2024/02/29/rishi-sunak-calls-in-university-leaders-after-warning-uk-is-descending-into-mob-rule/
Eagleton, T. (1991). *Ideology: An Introduction.* Verso books.
Edwards, K. (2004). The university in Europe and the US. In R. King (Ed.), *The University in the Global Age* (pp. 27–44). Palgrave Macmillan.
Edwards, T. J., & Miller, H. (1998). Change in mass higher education: University, state and economy. In D. Jary & M. Parker (Eds.), *The New Higher Education: Issues and Directions for the Post- Dearing University* (pp. 41–62). Staffordshire University Press.
Elsom, J. 2023. Course of Action Slashing immigration must come before propping up 'failing' universities, Tories warn. *The Sun,* July 3. Retrieved April 24, 2024, from https://www.thesun.co.uk/news/politics/22912345/slashing-immigration-must-come-before-unis/
Evans, G. R. (2018). University': The history of the search for a definition in England. In M. Feingold (Ed.), *History of Universities: Volume XXXI* (pp. 187–212). Oxford University Press.
Evans, P., & Sewell, W. H. (2013). Neoliberalism: Policy regimes, international regimes, and social effects. In P. Hall & M. Lamont (Eds.), *Social Resilience in the Neoliberal Era* (pp. 35–68). Cambridge University Press.

Fabricant, M., & Brier, S. (2016). *Austerity Blues: Fighting for the Soul of Public Higher Education*. Johns Hopkins University Press.

Fazackerley, A. (2023). Top universities 'will turn away more UK students' as fees fail to match costs. *The Guardian*, July 29. Retrieved April 24, 2024, from https://www.theguardian.com/education/2023/jul/29/top-universities-will-turn-away-more-uk-students-as-fees-fail-to-match-costs

Feenberg, A. (2014). *The Philosophy of Praxis: Marx, Lukács and the Frankfurt School*. Verso books.

Feola, R., Parente, R., & Cucino, V. (2021). The entrepreneurial university: How to develop the entrepreneurial orientation of academia. *Journal of the Knowledge Economy*, 12(4), 1787–1808.

Ferlie, E., Musselin, C., & Andresani, G. (2009). The governance of higher education systems: A public management perspective. In C. Paradeise, E. Reale, I. Bleiklie, & E. Ferlie (Eds.), *University Governance: Western European Comparative Perspective* (pp. 1–19). Springer.

Feser, E. (2006). *Cambridge Companion to Hayek Cambridge*. Cambridge University Press.

Fitz, J., & Hafid, T. (2007). Perspectives on the privatization of public schooling in England and Wales. *Educational Policy*, 21(1), 273–296.

Fleming, P. (2021). The ghost university: Academe from the ruins. *Emancipations: A Journal of Critical Social Analysis*, 1(1) article 4.

Flew, T. (2012). Michel Foucault's the birth of biopolitics and contemporary neoliberalism debates. *Thesis Eleven*, 108(1), 47–65.

Flew, T. (2014). Six theories of neoliberalism. *Thesis Eleven*, 122(1), 49–71.

Foskett, N. (2011). Markets, government, funding and the marketisation of higher education. In M. Molesworth, R. Scullion, & E. Nixon (Eds.), *The Marketisation of Higher Education and the Student* (pp. 25–38). Routledge.

Foster, P. (2023). UK universities urged to cut 'fraudulent' international student applications. *Financial Times*, October 19. Retrieved April 24, 2024, from https://www.ft.com/content/d60acbb1-49cc-4a3f-805a-4cee6c320370

Foucault, M. (1977). *Discipline and Punish: The Birth of the Prison*. Penguin.

Foucault, M. (1978). *The history of sexuality volume 1: An introduction* (R. Hurley, Trans.). Pantheon Books.

Foucault, M. (1981). *The will to knowledge: The history of sexuality, Vol. 1*. Penguin.

Foucault, M. (1988). Technologies of the self. In L. H. Martin, H. Gutman, & P. H. Hutton (Eds.), *Technologies of the self* (pp. 16–49). University of Massachusetts Press.

Foucault, M. (1994). The subject and power. In J. D. Faubion (Ed.), *Michel Foucault – Power: The essential works of Foucault, vol. 3* (pp. 327–348). Penguin.

Foucault, M. (2008). *The Birth of Biopolitics: Lectures at the Collège de France, 1978–79*. Palgrave.

Frank, J., Gowar, N., & Naef, M. (2019). *English universities in crisis: Markets without competition*. Bristol University Press.

Friedman, M. (1955). The role of government in education. In R. A. Solo (Ed.), *Economics and the public interest* (pp. 85–107). Rutgers University Press.

Friedman, M. (1962). *Capitalism and Freedom*. University of Chicago Press.

Gamble, A. (2001). Neo-liberalism. *Capital and Class, 25*(1), 127–134.

Gane, M. (2008). Foucault on governmentality and liberalism. *Theory, Culture & Society, 25*(7–8), 353–363.

Gane, N. (2012). The Governmentalities of Neoliberalism: Panopticism, post-panopticism and beyond. *The Sociological Review, 60*(4), 611–634.

Gane, N. (2020). Competition: A critical history of a concept. *Theory, Culture & Society, 37*(2), 31–59.

Gerrard, J. (2015). Public education in neoliberal times: Memory and desire. *Journal of Education Policy, 30*(6), 855–868.

Gerstle, G. (2022). *The Rise and Fall of the Neoliberal Order: America and the World in the Free Market Era*. Oxford University Press.

Gewirtz, S., Ball, S., & Bowe, R. (1995). *Markets, choice, and equity in education*. Open University Press.

Gibbs, P. (2001). Higher education as a market: A problem or solution? *Studies in Higher Education, 26*(1), 85–94.

Gilbert, J. (2013). What kind of thing is "neoliberalism"? *New Formations: A Journal of Culture/Theory/Politics, 80*(80), 7–22.

Ginsberg, B. (2011). *The fall of the faculty: The rise of the all-administrative university and why it matters*. Oxford University Press.

Giroux, H. A. (2007). *The University in Chains: Confronting the Military-Industrial-Academic Complex*. Paradigm.

Giroux, H. A. (2008). Beyond Biopolitics of disposability: Rethinking neoliberalism in the New Gilded Age. *Social Identities, 14*(5), 587–620.

Giroux, H. A. (2010). Bare pedagogy and the scourge of neoliberalism: Rethinking higher education as a democratic public sphere. *The Educational Forum, 74*(3), 184–196.

Giroux, H. A. (2014). *Neoliberalism's War on Higher Education*. Haymarket Books.

Giroux, H. A., & Giroux, S. S. (2004). *Take Back Higher Education*. Palgrave Macmillan.

Gray, J., O'Regan, J. P., & Wallace, C. (2018). Education and the discourse of global neoliberalism. *Language and Intercultural Communication, 18*(5), 471–477.

Greener, I. (2008). Choice and voice – a review. *Social Policy and Society, 7*(2), 255–265.

Gruber, T. (2014). Academic sell-out: How an obsession with metrics and rankings is damaging academia. *Journal of Marketing for Higher Education, 24*(2), 165–177.

Gruening, G. (2001). Origin and theoretical basis of new public management. *International Public Management Journal*, 4(1), 1–25.
Habermas, J. (1987a). The university in a democracy: Democratization of the university. In *Toward a Rational Society* (pp. 1–12). Polity Press.
Habermas, J. (1987b). The Idea of the University – Learning Processes. *New German Critique*, 41, 3–22.
Hall, S. (1988). *Thatcherism and the Crisis of the Left: The Hard Road to Renewal*. Verso.
Hall, S. (2011). The neoliberal revolution. *Soundings*, 48, 9–28.
Hall, S., D. Massey, D. and M. Rustin, M. 2013. After neoliberalism: Analysing the present. *Soundings*, 53: 8–22.
Hardin, C. (2014). Finding the 'Neo' in neoliberalism. *Cultural Studies*, 28(2), 199–221.
Harvey, D. (2006). *A Brief History of Neoliberalism*. Oxford University Press.
Hayek, F. (1945a). The use of knowledge in society. *American Economic Review*, 35(4), 519–530.
Hayek, F. (2006a). *The Constitution of Liberty*. Routledge.
Hayek, F. A. (1944). *The Road to Serfdom*. Routledge & Kegan Paul.
Hayek, F. A. (1948). *Individualism and Economic Order*. University of Chicago Press.
Hayek, F. A. (1967). *Studies in Philosophy, Politics and Economics*. Routledge.
Hayek, F. A. (1973). *Law, Legislation & Liberty, Volume 1: Rules and Order*. Routledge & Kegan Paul.
Hayek, F. A. (2002). Competition as a discovery procedure. *Quarterly Journal of Austrian Economics*, 5(3), 9–23.
Hazelkorn, E. (2015). *Rankings and the Reshaping of Higher Education: The Battle for World-Class Excellence* (2nd ed.). Palgrave Macmillan.
Heller, H. (2016). *The Capitalist University: The Transformations of Higher Education in the United States since 1945*. Pluto Press.
Hemsley-Brown, J. (2011). Market heal thyself: The challenges of a free market in higher education. *Journal of Marketing for Higher Education*, 21(2), 115–132.
Henkel, M. (1997). Academic values and the university as corporate enterprise. *Higher Education Quarterly*, 51(2), 134–143.
Henry, G. (2002). Neoliberalism, corporate culture, and the promise of higher education: The university as a democratic public sphere. *Harvard Educational Review*, 72(4), 425–464.
Henry, G. A. (2012). *Disposable Youth: Racialized Memories, and the Culture of Cruelty*. Routledge.
Henry, J. (2023). Immigration chiefs warn universities after thousands of foreign students claim asylum within months of arriving in Britain. *Daily Mail*, October 28. Retrieved April 24, 2024, from https://www.dailymail.co.uk/news/arti-

cle-12683921/Immigration-chiefs-warn-universities-thousands-foreign-students-claim-asylum-months-arriving-Britain.html
Hill, D. (2003). Global neo-liberalism, the deformation of education and resistance. *The Journal of Critical Education Policy Studies, 1*(1), 1–28.
Hill, D., & Kumar, R. (Eds.). (2011). *Global Neoliberalism and Education and its Consequences*. Routledge.
Hillman, N. (2016). The Coalition's higher education reforms in England. *Oxford Review of Education, 42*(3), 330–345.
Hindess, B. (1996). *Discourses of Power: From Hobbes to Foucault*. Blackwell.
HM Government. (2004). *Higher Education Act*. HMSO.
Holmwood, J. (Ed.). (2011). *A Manifesto for the Public University*. Bloomsbury.
Holmwood, J. (2014). From social rights to the market: Neoliberalism and the knowledge economy. *International Journal of Lifelong Education, 33*(1), 62–76.
https://www.theguardian.com/news/2017/aug/18/neoliberalism-the-idea-that-changed-the-world
https://www.thenationalnews.com/world/uk-news/2024/02/29/rishi-sunak-calls-in-university-leaders-after-warning-uk-is-descending-into-mob-rule/
Hunt, S. A., & Boliver, V. (2023). The private higher education provider landscape in the UK. *Studies in Higher Education, 48*(9), 1346–1360.
Hursh, D. (2005). Neo-liberalism, markets and accountability: Transforming education and undermining democracy in the United States and England. *Policy Futures in Education, 3*(1), 3–15.
Hursh, D. W., & Henderson, J. A. (2011). Contesting global neoliberalism and creating alternative futures. *Discourse: Studies in the Cultural Politics of Education, 32*(2), 171–185.
Ingleby, E. (2021). *Neoliberalism Across Education: Policy and Practice from Early Childhood Through Adult Learning*. Palgrave Macmillan.
Jackson, B., & Saunders, R. (2012). *Making Thatcher's Britain*. Cambridge University Press.
Jarrat, A. (1985). *Report of the Steering Committee for Efficiency Studies in Universities*. HMSO.
Jaspers, K. (1961). *The Idea of a University*. Peter Owen.
John, P., & Fanghanel, J. (Eds.). (2016). *Dimensions of Marketisation in Higher Education*. Routledge.
John, P., & Fanghanel, J. (2015). 'Fearful symmetry?' Higher education and the logic of the market. In P. John & J. Fanghanel (Eds.), *Dimensions of Marketisation in Higher Education* (pp. 1–12). Routledge.
Jones, B. M. A., & Ball, S. J. (2023). *Neoliberalism and Education*. Routledge.
Jones, S., Vigurs, K., & Harris, D. (2020). Discursive framings of market-based education policy and their negotiation by students: The case of 'value for money' in English universities. *Oxford Review of Education, 46*(3), 375–392.

Jongbloed, B. (2003). Marketisation in higher education, Clark's triangle and the essential ingredients of markets. *Higher Education Quarterly, 57*(2), 110–135.

Kallio, K.-M., Kallio, T. J., Tienari, J., & Hyvönen, T. (2016). Ethos at stake: Performance management and academic work in universities. *Human Relations, 69*(3), 685–709.

Karlin, M. (2018). Henry A. Giroux: The nightmare of neoliberal fascism. Truthout, June 10. Retrieved April 22, 2024, from https://truthout.org/articles/henry-a-giroux-the-nightmare-of-neoliberal-fascism/

Kelly, P., Fair, N., & Evans, C. (2017). The engaged student ideal in UK higher education policy. *High Education Policy, 30*, 105–122.

Kerr, C. (1963). *The Uses of the University*. Harvard University Press.

Kezar, A. (2004). Obtaining integrity? Reviewing and examining the charter between higher education and society. *The Review of Higher Education, 27*(4), 429–459.

Kezar, A., Scott, D., & DePaola, T. (2019). *The Gig Academy: Mapping Labor in the Neoliberal University*. John Hopkins University Press.

Kiely, R. (2018). *The Neoliberal Paradox*. Edward Elgar.

King, R. (2003). *The University in the Global Age*. Palgrave Macmillan.

Klees, S. J. (2008). A quarter century of neoliberal thinking in education: Misleading analyses and failed policies. *Globalisation, Societies, and Education, 6*(4), 311–348.

Klein, N. (2007). *The Shock Doctrine: The Rise of Disaster Capitalism*. Metropolitan Books/Henry Holt.

Klepeis, P., & Vance, C. (2003). Neoliberal policy and deforestation in southeastern Mexico: An assessment of the PROCAMPO program. *Economic Geography, 79*(3), 221–240.

Klikauer, T. (2013). *Managerialism: A Critique of an Ideology*. Palgrave Macmillan.

Knafo, S., Dutta, S. J., Lane, R., Wyn-Jones, S., & S. (2019). The managerial lineages of neoliberalism. *New Political Economy, 24*(2), 235–251.

Knights, D., & Clarke, C. A. (2014). It's a bittersweet symphony, this life: Fragile academic selves and insecure identities at work. *Organization Studies, 35*(3), 335–357.

Komljenovic, J. (2020). Commodifying higher education: The proliferation of devices for making markets. In C. Callender, W. Locke, & S. Marginson (Eds.), *Changing Higher Education for a Changing World* (pp. 191–204). Bloomsbury.

Krause-Jensen, J., & Garsten, C. (2014a). Introduction: Neoliberal turns in higher education. *Learning and Teaching, 7*(3), 1–13.

Krippner, G. (2011). *Capitalizing on Crisis: The Political Origins of the Rise of Finance*. Harvard University Press.

Laclau, E., & Mouffe, C. (1985). *Hegemony and socialist strategy: Towards a radical democratic politics* (2nd ed.). Verso books.

Lambert, H. (2019). The great university con: How the British degree lost its value. *The New Statesman*, August 13. Retrieved April 22, 2024, from https://www.newstatesman.com/politics/2019/08/the-great-university con-how-the-british-degree-lost-its-value

Larner, W. (2006). Review of *a brief history of neoliberalism*. *Economic Geography*, *82*, 449–451.

Le Grand, J. (2007). *The Other Invisible Hand: Delivering Public Services through Choice and Competition*. Princeton University Press.

Le Grand, J., & Bartlett, W. (1993). *Quasi-Markets and Social Policy*. Macmillan.

Levidow, L. (2005a). Neoliberal agendas for higher education. In A. Saad-Filho & D. Johnston (Eds.), *Neoliberalism: A Critical Reader* (pp. 156–163). Pluto Press.

Lipman, P. (2007). "No child left behind": Globalization, privatization, and the politics of inequality. In E. W. Ross & R. Gibson (Eds.), *Neoliberalism and Education Reform* (pp. 35–58). Hampton Press.

Lolich, L. (2011). ...and the market created the student to its image and likening. Neo-liberal governmentality and its effects on higher education in Ireland. *Irish Educational Studies*, *30*(2), 271–284.

Lovlie, L., & Standish, P. (2003). Introduction: Bildung and the idea of a liberal education. In L. Lovlie, K. P. Mortensenand, & S. E. Nordenbo (Eds.), *Educating Humanity: Bildung in Postmodernity* (pp. 1–24). Blackwell.

Lowe, R. (Ed.). (2008). *The History of Higher Education*. Routledge.

Lunt, I. (2008). Beyond tuition fees? The legacy of Blair's government to higher education. *Oxford Review of Education*, *34*(6), 741–752.

Lynch, K. (2006). Neo-liberalism and Marketisation: The implications for higher education. *European Educational Research Journal*, *5*(1), 1–17.

Lynch, K. (2014). "New managerialism" in education: The organisational form of neoliberalism'. *Open Democracy*, September 16. Retrieved April 24, 2024, from https://www.opendemocracy.net/kathleen-lynch/'new-managerialism'-in-education-organisational-form-of-neoliberalism

Maisuria, A. (2014). The neo-liberalisation policy agenda and its consequences for education in England: A focus on resistance now and possibilities for the future. *Policy Futures in Education*, *12*(2), 286–296.

Maisuria, A., & Cole, M. (2017). The neoliberalization of higher education in England: An alternative is possible. *Policy Futures in Education*, *15*(5), 602–619.

Mandler, P. (2020). *The Crisis of the Meritocracy. Britain's Transition to Mass Education Since the Second World War*. Oxford University Press.

Mandler, P. (2022). *The Crisis of the Meritocracy. Britain's Transition to Mass Education Since the Second World War*. Oxford University Press. 2020.

Marginson, S. (1997). *Markets in Education*. Allen and Unwin.

Marginson, S. (2006). Dynamics of national and global competition in higher education. *Higher Education*, *52*(1), 1–39.

Marginson, S. (2008). Global field and global imagining: Bourdieu and worldwide higher education. *British Journal of Sociology of Education, 29*(3), 303–315.
Marginson, S. (2013). The impossibility of capitalist markets in higher education. *Journal of Education Policy, 28*(3), 353–370.
Marginson, S. (2017). The World-Class Multiversity: Global commonalities and national characteristics. *Frontiers of Education in China, 12,* 233–260.
Marginson, S. (2018). Public/private in higher education: A synthesis of economic and political approaches. *Studies in Higher Education, 43*(2), 322–337.
Marx, K., & Engels, F. (1970). *The German ideology: Part one.* International Publishers.
Matutinovic, I. (2020). The end of neoliberal ideology. *Green European Journal.* Retrieved April 24, 2024, from https://www.greeneuropeanjournal.eu/the-end-of-neoliberal-ideology/
Mavelli, L. (2022). *Neoliberal Citizenship: Sacred Markets, Sacrificial Lives.* Oxford University Press.
Mayhew, K., Deer, C., & Dua, M. (2004). The move to mass higher education in the UK: Many questions and some answers. *Oxford Review of Education, 30*(1), 65–82.
McCaig, C. (2018). *The Marketisation of English Higher Education: A Policy Analysis of a Risk-based System.* Emerald.
McCulloch, A. (2009). The student as co-producer: Learning from public administration about the student-university relationship. *Studies in Higher Education, 34*(2), 171–183.
McGettigan, A. (2013). *The Great University Gamble: Money, Markets and the Future of Higher Education.* Pluto Press.
McGuigan, J. (2016). *Neoliberal Culture.* Palgrave Macmillan.
McLaren, P. (2005a). *Capitalist and Conquerors: A Critical Pedagogy Against Empire.* Rowman & Littlefield.
Metcalf, S. (2017). Neoliberalism: The idea that swallowed the world. *The Guardian,* August 18. Retrieved April 22, 2024, from https://www.theguardian.com/news/2017/aug/18/neoliberalism-the-idea-that-changed-the-world
Mikhailova, A. (2022). Education secretary Nadhim Zahawi plans crackdown on 'Mickey Mouse' degrees – with universities required to publish drop-out rate and graduate job outcomes on every advert. *Daily Mail,* March 20. Retrieved April 24, 2024, from https://www.dailymail.co.uk/news/article-10631871/Education-Secretary-Nadhim-Zahawi-plans-crackdown-Mickey-Mouse-degrees.html
Mincer, J. (1974). *Schooling, Experience, and Earnings* (p. 1974). Columbia University Press.
Mintz, B. (2021). Neoliberalism and the crisis in higher education: The cost of ideology. *American Journal of Economics and Sociology, 80*(1), 79–112.

Mirowski, P. (2013). *Never Let a Serious Crisis Go to Waste: How Neoliberalism Survived the Financial Meltdown*. Verso books.
Mirowski, P., Plehwe, D., & D. (2009). *The Road from Mont Pèlerin: The Making of the Neoliberal Thought Collective*. Harvard University Press.
Mises, L. (1944). *Bureaucracy*. Yale University Press.
Mises, von, L. (2007). *Human Action*. Liberty Fund.
Molesworth, M., Scullion, R., & Nixon, E. (Eds.). (2010). *The Marketisation of Higher Education: The Student as Consumer*. Routledge.
Moore, R. (2021). The free-market gamble: Has Covid broken UK universities? *The Guardian*, January 17. Retrieved April 24, 2024, from https://www.theguardian.com/education/2021/jan/17/free-market-gamble-has-covid-broken-uk-universities
Morgan, H. (2022). Neoliberalism's influence on American universities: How the business model harms students and society. *Policy Futures in Education, 20*(2), 149–165.
Morrissey, J. (2013). Governing the academic subject: Foucault, governmentality and the performing university. *Oxford Review of Education, 39*(6), 797–810.
Mudge, S. L. (2008). The state of the art: What is neo-liberalism? *Socio-Economic Review, 6*(4), 703–731.
Musselin, C. (2018). New forms of competition in higher education. *Socio-Economic Review, 16*(3), 657–683.
Naidoo, R., & Jamieson, I. (2005). Empowering participants or corroding learning: Towards a research agenda on the impact of student consumerism in higher education. *Journal of Education Policy, 20*(3), 267–281.
Naidoo, R., Shankar, A., & Veer, E. (2011). The consumerist turn in higher education: Policy aspirations and outcomes. *Journal of Marketing Management, 27*(11–12), 1142–1162.
Naidoo, R., & Williams, J. (2015). The neoliberal regime in English higher education: charters, consumers and the erosion of the public good. *Critical Studies in Education, 56*(2), 208–223.
Nairn, K., & Higgins, J. (2007). New Zealand's neoliberal generation: Tracing discourses of economic (ir) rationality. *International Journal of Qualitative Studies in Education, 20*(3), 261–281.
Nash, K. (2019). Neo-liberalisation, universities and the values of bureaucracy. *The Sociological Review, 67*(1), 178–193.
Natale, S. M., & Doran, C. (2012). Marketisation of education: An ethical dilemma. *Journal of Business Ethics, 105*(2), 187–196.
Newfield, C. (2011). *Unmaking the Public University: The Forty-Year Assault on the Middle Class*. Harvard University Press.
Newman, J. H. (1996). *The Idea of a University*. Mcmackin Garland, M. et al. (eds.): Yale University Press.

Newman, S., & Jahdi, K. (2009). Marketisation of education: Marketing, rhetoric and reality. *Journal of Further and Higher Education, 33*(1), 1–11.

Nik-Khah, E., van Horn, R., & R. (2016). The ascendancy of Chicago neoliberalism. In S. Springer, K. Birch, & J. MacLeavy (Eds.), *The Handbook of Neoliberalism* (pp. 27–38). Routledge.

Nixon, E., Scullion, R., & Hearn, R. (2018). Her majesty the student: Marketised higher education and the narcissistic (dis)satisfactions of the student-consumer. *Studies in Higher Education, 43*(6), 927–943.

Nonini, D. (2008). Is China becoming neoliberal? *Critique of Anthropology, 28*(2), 145–176.

Nordbäck, E., Hakonen, M., Tienari, J., & J. (2022). Academic identities and sense of place: A collaborative autoethnography in the neoliberal university. *Management Learning, 53*(2), 331–349.

Nussbaum, M. C. (1997). *Cultivating Humanity: A Classical Defense of Reform in Liberal Education*. Harvard University Press.

O'Day, R. (2009). Universities and Professions in the early modern period. In P. Cunningham, S. Oosthuizen, & R. Taylor (Eds.), *Beyond the Lecture Hall Universities and community engagement from the middle ages to the present day* (pp. 79–102). University of Cambridge Faculty of Education and Institute of Continuing Education.

Office for Students (OfS). (2019). Office for Students' value for money strategy 2019 to 2021. Retrieved April 24, 2024, from https://www.officeforstudents.org.uk/media/336c258b-d94c-4f15-af0a-42e1be8f66a1/ofs-vfm-strategy.pdf

Olssen, M. (2000). The neo-liberal appropriation of tertiary education policy: Accountability, research and academic freedom. *Access: Contemporary Issues in Education, 19*(2), 142–188.

Olssen, M. (2001). *The Neo-liberal Appropriation of Tertiary Education Policy: Accountability, Research and Academic Freedom. State-of-the-Art Monograph, no. 8, October*. New Zealand Association for Research in Education.

Olssen, M., Codd, J., & O'Neill, A.-M. (2004). *Education Policy: Globalization, Citizenship and Democracy*. Sage.

Olssen, M., & Peters, M. A. (2005). Neoliberalism, higher education and the knowledge economy: From the free market to knowledge capitalism. *Journal of Education Policy, 20*(3), 313–345.

O'Malley, P. (1992). Risk, power and crime prevention. *Economy & Society, 21*(3), 252–275.

Ong, A. (2006). *Neoliberalism as Exception: Mutations in Citizenship and Sovereignty*. Duke University Press.

Overbeek, H., & Van Apeldoorn, B. (2012). *Neoliberalism in Crisis*. Palgrave Macmillan.

PA media. (2022). Sharp rise in top degrees at three English universities investigated. *The Guardian*, September 2. Retrieved April 24, 2024, from https://www.theguardian.com/education/2022/sep/02/office-for-students-investigates-sharp-rise-top-degrees-universities

Palfreyman, D., & Tapper, T. (2014). *Reshaping the University: The Rise of the Regulated Market in Higher Education*. Oxford University Press.

Parker, L. D. (2022). Public university research engagement contradictions in a commercialisation higher education world. *Financial Accountability & Management, 40*(1), 1–18.

Parker, M., & Jary, D. (1995). The McUniversity: Organisations, management and academic subjectivity'. *Organization, 2*(2), 319–338.

Peck, J. (2008). Remaking laissez-faire. *Progress in Human Geography, 32*(1), 3–43.

Peck, J. (2010). *Constructions of Neoliberal Reason*. Oxford University Press.

Peck, J. (2013). Explaining (with) neoliberalism. *Territory, Politics, Governance, 1*(2), 132–157.

Peck, J. (2015). (Neo) liberalism, popular media, and the political struggle for the future of US-public education. *European Journal of Communication, 30*(5), 587–603.

Peck, J., Brenner, N., & Theodore, N. (2018). Actually existing neoliberalism. In D. Cahill, M. Cooper, M. Konings, & D. Primrose (Eds.), *The Sage Handbook of Neoliberalism* (pp. 3–15). Sage.

Peck, J., & Theodore, N. (2015). *Fast policy: Experimental statecraft at the thresholds of neoliberalism*. University of Minnesota Press.

Peck, J., & Theodore, N. (2019). Still neoliberalism? *South Atlantic Quarterly, 118*(2), 245–265.

Peck, J., & Tickell, T. A. (2002). Neoliberalizing space. *Antipode, 34*(3), 380–404.

Pedersen O. 1998. *The First Universities: Studium Generale and the Origins of University Education in Europe*. North R, trans. Cambridge: Cambridge University Press.

Perera, M. (2023). Minister asks universities to adopt Mental Health Charter by September 2024 or face licensing restrictions. *Epigram*, June 12. Retrieved April 24, 2024, from https://epigram.org.uk/minister-asks-universities-to-adopt-mental-health-charter-by-september-2024-or-face-licensing-restrictions/

Perkin, H. (2007). History of universities. In J. J. F. Forest & P. G. Altbach (Eds.), *Handbook of Higher Education* (pp. 159–206). Springer.

Peters, A. M. & R. Barnett (Eds.). (2018). *The Idea of the University: A Reader (Vol. I)*. Peter Lang.

Peters, M. A. (2001). Foucault and governmentality: Understanding the neoliberal paradigm of education policy. *The School Field, 12*(5/6), 61–72.

Peters, M. A. (2003). Truth-telling as an educational practice of the self: Foucault, parrhesia and the ethics of subjectivity. *Oxford Review of Education, 29*(2), 207–223.

Peters, M. A. (2005). The new prudentialism in education: Actuarial rationality and the entrepreneurial self. *Educational Theory, 55*(2), 123–137.

Peters, M. A. (2017). From state responsibility for education and welfare to self-responsibilisation in the market. *Discourse: Studies in the Cultural Politics of Education, 38*(1), 138–145.

Peters, M. A., & Jandric, P. (2018). Neoliberalism and the university. In D. Cahill, M. Cooper, M. Konings, & D. Primrose (Eds.), *The Sage Handbook of Neoliberalism* (pp. 553–564). Sage.

Plehwe, D., Walpen, B., & Neunhoffer, G. (2006). Introduction: Reconsidering neoliberal hegemony. In D. Plehwe, B. Walpen, & G. Neunhoffer (Eds.), *Neoliberal Hegemony: A Global Critique* (pp. 1–24). Routledge.

Potts, M. (2005). The consumerist subversion of education. *Academic Questions, 18*(3), 54–64.

Prasad, M. (2006). *The Politics of Free Markets: The Rise of Neoliberal Economic Policies in Britain, France, Germany and the United States*. University of Chicago.

Pratt, N. (2016). Neoliberalism and the (internal) marketisation of primary school assessment in England. *British Educational Research Journal, 42*(5), 890–905.

Pusser, B. (2006). Reconsidering higher education and the public good: The role of public spheres. In W. G. Tierney (Ed.), *Governance and the Public Good* (pp. 11–28). State University of New York Press.

Pusser, B., & Marginson, S. (2013). University rankings in critical perspective. *Higher Education, 84*(4), 544–568.

Radice, H. (2015). How we got here: UK higher education under neoliberalism. *ACME: An International Journal for Critical Geographies, 12*(2), 407–418.

Ranson, S. (2003). Public accountability in the age of neo-liberal governance. *Journal of Education Policy, 18*(5), 459–480.

Readings, B. (1996). *The University in Ruins*. Harvard University Press.

Rhoades, R., Sporn, B., & B. (2002). Quality assurance in Europe and the US: Professional and political economic framing of higher education policy. *Higher Education, 43*(3), 355–390.

Robbins, L. (1963). *Higher Education: Report of the Committee Appointed by the Prime Minister under the Chairmanship of Lord Robbins, Cmnd. 2154*. HMSO.

Robertson, S. (2000). *A Class Act Changing Teachers Work, the State, and Globalisation*. Falmer.

Rose, N. (1993). Government, authority and expertise in advanced liberalism. *Economy & Society, 22*(3), 283–299.

Rose, N. (1996). *Inventing Our Selves*. Cambridge University Press.

Rose, N. (1999). *Powers of Freedom: Reframing Political Thought*. Cambridge University Press.
Rothblatt, S. (1997). *The Modern University and its Discontents: The Fate of Newman's Legacies in Britain and America*. Cambridge University Press.
Rowlands, J., Rawolle, S., & S. (2013). Neoliberalism is not a theory of everything: A Bourdieuian analysis of illusio in educational research. *Critical Studies in Education, 54*(3), 260–272.
Rustin, M. (2016). The neoliberal university and its alternatives. *Soundings, 63*(63), 147–176.
Salter, B., & Tapper, T. (1994). *The State and Higher Education*. The Woburn Press.
Sanderson, M. (1972). *The Universities and British Industry 1850–1970*. Routledge & Kegan Paul.
Saunders, D. B. (2010). Neoliberal ideology and public higher education in the United States. *Journal for Critical Education Policy Studies, 8*(1), 41–77.
Schmidt, V. (2018). Ideas and the rise of neoliberalism in Europe. In D. Cahill, M. Cooper, M. Konings, & D. Primrose (Eds.), *The Sage Handbook of Neoliberalism* (pp. 69–81). Sage.
Schraedley, M. A., Jenkins, J. J., Irelan, M., & Umana, M. (2021). The neoliberalization of higher education: Paradoxing students' basic needs at a hispanic-serving institution. *Frontiers in Sustainable Food Systems, 5*(689499), 1–13.
Schram, S. (2015). *The Return of Ordinary Capitalism: Neoliberalism, Precarity, Occupy*. Oxford University Press.
Schulze-Cleven, T., Reitz, T., & Maesse, J. et al. (2017). The new political economy of higher education: between distributional conflicts and discursive stratification. *Higher Education 73*, 795–812.
Scott, P. (2016). Private commodities and public goods: Markets and values in higher education. In P. John & J. Fanghanel (Eds.), *Dimensions of marketisation in higher education* (pp. 15–25). Routledge.
Scott, P. (2021). *Retreat or Resolution? Tackling the Crisis of Mass Higher Education*. University of Bristol Press.
Shattock, M. (2008). The change from private to public governance of British higher education: Its consequences for higher education policy making 1980–2006. *Higher Education Quarterly, 62*(3), 181–203.
Shattock, M. (2012). *Making Policy in British Higher Education: 1945–2011*. Routledge.
Shattock, M. (2013). University governance, leadership and management in a decade of diversification and Uncertainty. *Higher Education Quarterly, 67*(3), 217–233.
Shattock, M., & Horvath, A. (2020). *The Governance of British Higher Education the Impact of Governmental, Financial and Market Pressures*. Bloomsbury.

Shepherd, S. (2018). Managerialism: An ideal type. *Studies in Higher Education*, 43(9), 1668–1678.
Shields, R., & Watermeyer, R. (2020). Competing institutional logics in universities in the United Kingdom: Schism in the church of reason. *Studies in Higher Education*, 45(1), 3–17.
Shore, C., & Wright, S. (2004). Whose accountability? Governmentality and the auditing of universities. *Parallax*, 10(2), 100–116.
Skålén, P. (2009). Service marketing and subjectivity: The shaping of customer-oriented proactive employees. *Journal of Marketing Management*, 25(7–8), 795–809.
Skålén, P. (2010). *Managing Service Firms: The Power of Managerial Marketing*. Routledge.
Slaughter, S., and G. Rhoades. 2000. The neo-liberal university. *New Labor Forum*, 6(Spring–Summer), 73–79.
Slaughter, S., & Rhoades, G. (2004a). *Academic Capitalism and the New Economy: Markets, State and Higher Education*. Johns Hopkins University Press.
Slaughter, S., & Rhoades, G. (2004b). *Academic Capitalism and the New Economy: Markets, Ideology*. Palgrave Macmillan.
Slobodian, Q. (2018). *Globalists: The End of Empire and the Birth of Neoliberalism*. Harvard University Press.
Smart, B. (2003). *Economy, Culture and Society: A Sociological Critique of Neoliberalism*. Open University Press.
Smyth, J. (2017). *The Toxic University: Zombie Leadership, Academic Rock Stars, and Neoliberal State and Higher Education*. Palgrave MacMillan.
Sørensen, A. (2015). From critique of ideology to politics: Habermas on Bildung. *Ethics and Education*, 10(2), 252–270.
Sousa, C. A., de Nijs, W. F., & Hendriks, P. H. (2010). Secrets of the beehive: Performance management in university research organizations. *Human Relations*, 63(9), 1439–1460.
Spohrer, K. (2011). Deconstructing 'Aspiration': UK policy debates and European policy trends. *European Educational Research Journal*, 10(1), 53–63.
Springer, S. (2012). Neoliberalism as discourse: Between Foucauldian political economy and Marxian poststructuralism. *Critical Discourse Studies*, 9(2), 133–147.
Springer, S. (2014). Postneoliberalism? *Review of Radical Political Economics*, 47(1), 5–17.
Springer, S. (2016). *The Discourse of Neoliberalism: An Anatomy of a Powerful Idea*. Rowman and Littlefield.
Stedman Jones, D. (2012). *Masters of the Universe: Hayek, Friedman, and the Birth of Neoliberal Politics*. Princeton University Press.
Steger, M. B., & Roy, R. K. (2010). *Neoliberalism: A Very Short Introduction*. Oxford University Press.

Stigler, G. (1957). Perfect competition, historically contemplated. *The Journal of Political Economy*, 65(1), 1–17.
Stiglitz, J. E. (2002). *Globalization and its Discontents*. Allen Lane/Penguin.
Tett, L., & Hamilton, M. (Eds.). (2021). *Resisting neoliberalism in education: Local, national and transnational perspectives*. Policy Press.
Tholen, G. (2014). *The Changing Nature of the Graduate Labour Market: Media, Policy and Political Discourses in the UK*. Palgrave Macmillan.
Tholen, G. (2017). *Graduate work: Skills, credentials, careers, and labour markets*. Oxford University Press.
Tholen, G. (2018). University isn't the be all and end all when it comes to employment outcomes. *The Conversation*, October 4. Retrieved April 24, 2024, from https://theconversation.com/university-isnt-the-be-all-and-end-all-when-it-comes-to-employment-outcomes-103180
Tholen, G. (2022). *Modern Work and the Marketisation of Higher Education*. Policy Press.
Thrift, N. (2005). *Knowing Capitalism*. Sage.
Tominey, C. (2022). Students should apply for refunds on their fees – at the end of the day, they're consumers. *The Telegraph*, January 21. Retrieved April 24, 2024, from https://www.telegraph.co.uk/education-and-careers/2022/01/21/students-should-apply-refunds-fees-end-day-consumers/
Tomlinson, M. (2017). Student perceptions of themselves as 'consumers' of higher education, British. *Journal of Sociology of Education*, 38(4), 450–467.
Tomlinson, S. (2001). Education policy, 1997–2000: The effects on top, bottom and middle England, International. *Studies in Sociology of Education*, 11(3), 261–278.
Torres, C. A. (2011). Public universities and the neoliberal common sense: Seven iconoclastic theses. *International Studies in Sociology of Education*, 21(3), 177–197.
Touraine, A. (2001). *Beyond Neoliberalism*. Polity.
Tribe, K. (2009). The political economy of modernity: Foucault's college de France lectures of 1978 and 1979. *Economy and Society*, 38(4), 679–698.
Troiani, I., & Dutson, C. (2021). The neoliberal university as a space to learn/think/work in higher education. *Architecture and Culture*, 9(1), 5–23.
Tullock, G. (1967). The welfare costs of tariffs, monopolies, and theft. *Western Economic Journal*, 5, 224–232.
UK Research and Innovation (UKRI). 2023. Research financial sustainability. https://www.ukri.org/publications/research-financial-sustainability-data/research-financial-sustainability-issues-paper/universities
van Andel, J., Pimentel Botas, C., Huisman, J., & J. (2012). The consumption values of and empowerment of student as customer in higher education: Taking a rational look inside 'Pandora's Box'. *Higher Education Review*, 45(1), 62–85.

van Horn, R., Mirowski, P., & Stapleford, T. A. (Eds.). (2013). *Building Chicago Economics: New Perspectives on the History of America's Most Powerful Economics Program*. Cambridge University Press.

Varman, R., Saha, B., & Skålén, P. (2011). Market subjectivity and neoliberal governmentality in higher education. *Journal of Marketing Management, 27*(11–12), 1163–1185.

Venugopal, R. (2015). Neoliberalism as concept. *Economy and Society, 44*(2), 165–187.

Vernon, J. (2018). The making of the neoliberal university in Britain. *Critical Historical Studies, 5*(2), 267–280.

Vican, S., Friedman, A., & Andreasen, R. (2020). Metrics, money, and managerialism: Faculty experiences of competing logics in higher education. *The Journal of Higher Education, 91*(1), 139–164.

Walton, J. K. (2011). The idea of the university. In M. Bailey & D. Freedman (Eds.), *The Assault on Universities* (pp. 15–26). Pluto.

Ward, K., & England, K. (2007). Introduction: Reading neoliberalization. In K. England & K. Ward (Eds.), *Neoliberalization: States, Networks, People* (pp. 1–22). Blackwell.

Watts, R. (2017). *Public Universities, Managerialism and the Value of Higher Education*. Palgrave Macmillan.

Weale, S. (2018). Student mental health must be top priority – universities minister. *The Guardian*, June 28. Retrieved April 24, 2024, from https://www.theguardian.com/education/2018/jun/28/student-mental-health-must-be-top-priority-universities-minister

Weale, S. (2019). DfE tells universities to stop 'unethical' admissions tactics. *The Guardian*, April 5. Retrieved April 24, 2024, from https://www.theguardian.com/education/2019/apr/05/dfe-tells-universities-to-stop-unethical-admissions-tactics

Weale, S. (2022). Students in England to pay back loans over 40 years instead of 30. *The Guardian*, February 24. Retrieved April 24, 2024, from https://www.theguardian.com/money/2022/feb/24/students-in-england-to-pay-back-loans-over-40-years-instead-of-30

Weale, S. (2023). Minister rules out lifting cap on student tuition fees in England. *The Guardian*, August 2. Retrieved April 24, 2024, from https://www.theguardian.com/education/2023/aug/02/minister-rules-out-lifting-cap-on-student-tuition-fees-in-england

Whitty, G. (2009). The legacy of neo-liberal school reform in England. *Comparative Education, 39*, 3–28.

Wilkins, A. (2012). The Spectre of Neoliberalism: Pedagogy, Gender and the construction of learner identities. *Critical Studies in Education, 53*(2), 197–210.

Willetts, D. (2017). *A University Education*. Oxford University Press.

Williams, G. (1997). The market route to mass higher education: British experience 1979–1996. *Higher Education Policy, 10*(3 4), 275–289.
Williams, G. (2004). The higher education market in the United Kingdom. In P. Teixeira, B. Jongbloed, D. Dill, & A. Amaral (Eds.), *Markets in Higer Education: Rhetoric or Reality?* (pp. 241–269). Springer.
Williams, G. (2013a). A bridge too far: An economic critique of marketization of higher education. In C. Callender & P. Scott (Eds.), *Browne and Beyond: Modernizing English Higher Education* (pp. 57–72). Institute of Education Press.
Williams, G. (2016a). Higher education: Public good or private commodity? *London Review of Education, 14*(1), 131–142.
Williams, J. (2013b). *Consuming Higher Education: Why Learning can't be Bought.* Bloomsbury.
Williams, J. (2016b). A critical exploration of changing definitions of public good in relation to higher education. *Studies in Higher Education, 41*(4), 619–630.
Wingate, S. (2022). Universities should limit 'low-quality' courses, minister says. *The Independent*, June 9. Retrieved April 24, 2024, from https://www.independent.co.uk/news/uk/universities-hepi-mental-health-nottingham-trent-university-government-b2097425.html
Yokoyama, K. (2008). Neo-liberal governmentality in the English and Japanese higher education. *International Studies in Sociology of Education, 18*(3), 231–247.

SPRINGER NATURE

GPSR Compliance

The European Union's (EU) General Product Safety Regulation (GPSR) is a set of rules that requires consumer products to be safe and our obligations to ensure this.

If you have any concerns about our products, you can contact us on ProductSafety@springernature.com

In case Publisher is established outside the EU, the EU authorized representative is:

Springer Nature Customer Service Center GmbH
Europaplatz 3
69115 Heidelberg, Germany

The manufacturer's authorised representative in the EU is Springer Nature Customer Service Centre GmbH, Europaplatz 3, 69115 Heidelberg, Germany. If you have any concerns regarding our products, please contact ProductSafety@springernature.com

Printed and bound by CPI Group (UK) Ltd, Croydon, CR0 4YY

23/03/2026

02076355-0011